Retrospectives on Switzerland in World War Two

Retrospectives on Switzerland in World War Two

Edited by
Donald P. Hilty

PICTON PRESS
ROCKPORT, MAINE

Library of Congress Cataloging-in-Publication Data

Retrospectives on Switzerland in World War Two / edited by Donald P.
Hilty.
    p. cm.
Most essays have been translated from German into English.
Most essays were originally published in a volume by Verlag Neue Zürcher
Zeitung under the title: Der Zweite Weltkrieg und die Schweiz. 1997.
Includes index.
    ISBN 0-89725-447-3 (hard cover : alk. paper)
    1. World War, 1939-1945— Switzerland. 2. Neutrality—
Switzerland— History— 20th century. 3. Switzerland— Economic policy.
4. Refugees, Jewish— Switzerland. I. Hilty, Donald P.
D754.S9 R48 2001
940.53'494--dc21   2001003994

Published under the auspices of the *American Swiss Foundation*.

First Printing November 2001

This book is available from:
Picton Press
PO Box 250
Rockport, ME 04856-0250

Visa/MasterCard orders: 1-207-236-6565
FAX orders: 1-207-236-6713
www.pictonpress.com

TABLE OF CONTENTS

Introduction
Donald P. Hilty v

Prologue: Swiss History under Scrutiny
Hugo Bütler ix

PART ONE: ECONOMY 1

I.   Switzerland's Foreign Trade Policy during World War II: Successful Perseverance of a Besieged Country,
Hans Schaffner 3

II.   Neutrality and Economic Warfare,
Klaus Urner 15

PART TWO: DEFENSE 61

III.   The Swiss Army was Ready: Reasons Germany Dropped "Operation Switzerland",
Hans Senn 63

IV.   Who Prolonged the Second World War?
Walther Hofer 76

PART THREE: POLITICS 85

V.   Neutral Switzerland – Humanitarian Switzerland: A Contradiction?
Hugo Bütler 87

VI.   Contested Swiss Neutrality,
Dietrich Schindler 91

VII.   Switzerland, International Law and World War II,
          Detlev F. Vagts 99

Epilogue: Summary View of Switzerland in World War II,
          Sigmund Widmer 117

Contributors and Acknowledgments 131

Index 135

INTRODUCTION

Researchers, opinion leaders, politicians and writers seeking a balanced view of Switzerland during World War II have access to very little relevant material published in English.[1] Given the limited material available in English, and the bias apparent in some of it, it is not surprising that some Americans refer negatively to Switzerland in discussions of World War II. Yet if Americans are to make the reasoned argument that Switzerland was not a Nazi collaborator, more information about the period must be available in English.

This book is intended to help fill this void by providing essays in English on a wide range of related subjects. Most of these essays were originally published in Switzerland in German. They are portrayals of Swiss thinking and behavior during World War II by authors who were either there at the time in responsible positions, or who are respected researchers of the period.

This is an eclectic book. The authors include publishers, historians, politicians, law professors and military strategists. Some of the essays are short, others long; some are the product of rigorous analysis; others were written for a more popular audience. So the offerings can be considered to include appetizers, main courses, coffee and desserts. All provide new facts and understanding in English about the environment of the time.

In the Prologue, Hugo Bütler, Chief Editor of the *Neue Zürcher Zeitung* (NZZ), expresses his opinion that the articles in this book deal with the main subjects about Switzerland's wartime past. He notes that the aim of this book is to provide diverse historical pictures that will withstand critical examination and thus serve as a basis for a dialogue about the country's past and future.

---

[1] These conclusions are based on extensive research by the author of this introduction using two basic guides: (1) Library of Congress collection–containing the largest number of Swiss titles outside Switzerland, and (2) Eureka Bibliographic File – an on-line record of materials at more than 1,000 leading U.S. libraries.

The main portion of this book is divided into three parts that define the main features of the Swiss environment during World War II. Essays in Part One are about the Economy, Part Two Defense, and Part Three Politics.

In the first essay in Part One, Hans Schaffner, former Director of the Central Office for War Economy, gives a firsthand description of the difficult tasks the foreign trade policy of any neutral country must fulfill during war times. His article shows how Swiss authorities and Swiss businesses were able to maintain trade with the most important countries despite blockades and counter-blockades.

Historian Klaus Urner wrote the second essay in Part One. He emphasizes how much the Swiss economy depends on trade. The country faced an economically difficult two-front war during World War II because of the pressures from Axis powers and from the Allies. He shows how Switzerland applied the rights and duties of economic neutrality to keep trade relations open with both sides and thereby to survive economically.

Part Two also includes two essays. Hans Senn, historian and former Chief of the General Staff of the Swiss Army, in the first essay answers the question: What military preparations did Switzerland make to restrain Nazi Germany from attacking? He concludes that the Swiss redoubt defense concept – the threat of a prolonged mountain war coupled with the destruction of alpine transit routes – maximized Swiss defense capabilities. He believes Swiss military capability played a key role in the "overall defense" of the country.

Walther Hofer, a prominent expert on the wartime era, wrote the second essay on defense. He rebuts the allegation in the Foreword to the Eizenstat Report that Switzerland's trade with Nazi Germany prolonged World War II. He argues that the premise is untenable and further argues that, if the game of hindsight is played, the Allied powers have much to explain.

Part Three is about politics. Editor Bütler, in his second essay, reasons that Switzerland's longstanding humanitarian tradition has been revitalized and reinforced through a large solidarity fund, a project of the Swiss Federal Council. He acknowledges that the project is still politically controversial and still uncertain, but rejects the idea it is a result of Swiss bad conscience or of American criticism of Swiss neutrality during World War II. Bütler feels humanitarian efforts and neutrality during both war and peace are closely linked.

University of Zürich Law Professor Dieter Schindler carefully examines the criticisms raised by U.S. Undersecretary of State Stuart E. Eizenstat, both in the Foreword and body of his report, about Swiss neutrality in World War II. Schindler recognizes opposing views. He is critical of Eizenstat's political assessments in the Foreword, yet admits Switzerland did not handle its neutrality impeccably in every respect. He concludes that the country faces the difficult task of resolving some issues about neutrality from the past while adapting its position of neutrality to present conditions.

In his rigorous analysis, Harvard Law School Professor Vagts concludes that the Swiss government's behavior during World War II was largely in compliance with the rules of international law, including the rules of neutrality. He found that some lapses in trade and transit occurred, although some of them were in favor of the Allies. He concludes that some gold transactions violated international law, but that a reasonable and binding settlement of these claims was achieved 50 years ago. He believes trespasses by other nations on Swiss rights as a neutral nation were more serious than the Swiss lapses. He notes that moral issues are more subjective than legal issues, and points to the familiar positive comments about Swiss actions during World War II by Churchill – who certainly knew the difficulties of governing during wartime.

Finally, former Zürich mayor Sigmund Widmer's essay serves as the epilogue. He recounts how Switzerland's geographical position – a small country caught between warring coalitions – pushed it over the centuries to adopt a policy of neutrality. Switzerland during World War II neither heroically sacrificed herself in the fight against tyranny, nor did she allow herself to be a willing partner of Nazi Germany. Switzerland stood by her neutrality in a bid for survival. He notes that a small minority of the people sympathized with Nazi Germany, but that the majority sympathized with the Allies. However, Switzerland was compelled to compromise (mainly in trade relations) with Germany and Italy for survival. While this compromise led to measures which can be criticized, these criticisms must be weighed against the remarkable feat of survival by a small democratic country encircled by dictators. This book seeks to offer an English-speaking audience a new understanding of that survival.

Several people made this book possible. Faith Whittlesey, former Ambassador of the United States to Switzerland and President of the American Swiss Foundation, generously gave the full support of her organization. George Gyssler, Chairman of the U.S. Advisory Council of the American Swiss Foundation, sparked it. He has a passion for publishing in the United States well-chosen classic Swiss history books in English. Professor of History, University of Illinois at Chicago, Leo Schelbert's fingerprints are all over this book. He gave generous amounts of translating, editing and organizing advice – always in his typical tireless and courteous manner. A list of contributors and specific acknowledgments are at the end of this book.

This book was funded in part by Presence Switzerland (PRS) and the Zuger Kulturstiftung Landis & Gyr, Zug, Switzerland and was published with the support of the Sophie and Karl Binding-Foundation, Basel, Switzerland.

Donald P. Hilty

PROLOGUE:

Swiss History under Scrutiny

Hugo Bütler

The recent debate about Switzerland's role in World War II and its conduct towards the Nazi powers and their victims during the war years and afterward reached an unexpected fierceness and depth. With the release of the so-called Eizenstat report by the Clinton administration it even grew into a conflict between the United States and Switzerland. The intensity of the dispute can only be understood in the context of this neutral country's unavoidable process of self-discovery, which re-emerged after the end of the bipolar East-West conflict.

Apart from a few new aspects, the dispute revives many topics which strongly occupied the Swiss and international public in the years immediately after the end of World War II. The neutral countries' actions with regard to their economic, financial, and gold policies during the years of mutual economic blockades by the nations at war led to difficult negotiations with the Allies in 1945/46 and to the Washington Agreement which included the agreement on payments by Switzerland to the Allies. After the capitulation, the Allies attempted to secure foreign or German assets looted by Hitler (e.g. plundered gold). The Swiss public, down to the smallest local newspaper, then intensively discussed the new payment of 1946 that had also considered those assets which Nazi leaders had transferred to Switzerland. Such payment was demanded because the moral standing of the neutrals that had survived the war unscathed and without direct military involvement was not particularly high in the eyes of the victorious Allies. In their fight against Hitler, the Allies had paid a high price in blood while Switzer-land had not taken sides in the fighting and now found itself confronted by numerous accusations and suspicions from the victors. Just as with the other neutral countries, the Swiss Confederation was not admitted to the founding conference of the United Nations in San Francisco. However Winston Churchill, the wartime British Prime Minister, viewed Switzerland's role most positively. He summarized his verdict as follows:

> Of all the neutrals Switzerland has the greatest right to distinction. She has been the sole international force linking the hideously sundered nations and ourselves. What does it matter whether she has been able to give us the commercial advantages we desire or has given too many to the Germans, to keep herself alive? She has been a democratic state, standing for freedom in self-defence among her mountains, and in thought, in spite of race, largely on our side.[1]

The public debate regarding the economic and moral role of the neutral country, however, was soon displaced internationally as well as nationally after 1946 by the hot subjects between East and West at the start of the Cold War. In this conflict freedom-loving and defense-ready Switzerland, which was then much involved in the emotional and material recovery of Europe, quickly assumed again the welcome position of an economically and politically reliable small country, even in the eyes of the United States and Great Britain. The majority of its people were now just as committed to the ideological defense against communist totalitarianism as it had been before to the moral and political resistance against the forces of Fascism and National Socialism. Not much changed until the earth-shaking events of 1989. The intensity of the East-West conflict, marked by the basic discourse of a polarized world, left few points of attack and not much room for a continued public debate about the weaknesses and problems of an isolated Switzerland which had been encircled by the Axis powers and stuck in the Alpine military redoubt during the worst years of World War II.

The political and moral collapse of the Soviet empire, the elimination of old threats and worries, the dismantling of the Iron Curtain, the opening of archives in Eastern Europe, the international commemoration of the fiftieth anniversary of the end of World War II shortly thereafter, the newly initiated international efforts regarding restitution of confiscated possessions and assets of Jewish citizens whom the Hitler regime had stripped of their rights (in Switzerland particularly: unclaimed bank

---

[1] Winston Churchill, *The Second World War*, Vol. 6: *Triumph and Tragedy* (1953), 712.

accounts), together with the cultural Holocaust debate since 1991 – all these developments prepared the terrain for a new discussion of Switzerland's role during World War II.

Irritated Sensibility of an Outsider Nation

The fact that the history of the country occupies Switzerland's public opinion with such intensity results also from internal changes within the country itself: the replacement of the political generation which for a long time shaped the influential thinking and judgment of the "generation of active servicemen" that is slowly fading away; the self-doubting of the political outsider who painfully searches for a path between neutrality and international cooperation, between a direct democracy that is strongly oriented towards domestic policy and political collaboration within an integrated Europe. This outsider, whose perpetual neutrality was recognized internationally in 1815 at the Congress of Vienna, vacillates today between the existence as a special case and as a new political normality. Added to this are economic uncertainties of a nation used to success in the export sector, but which now has painfully to adjust to economic globalization. To this must be added the pervasive inclination and readiness for self-incrimination in a media landscape which since 1968 shows a prevalent tendency to critically analyze the home country and its success, a tendency that is often greater than the desire for a just assessment of historical and political contexts. The weakness of the Federal Council's political leadership and the badly delayed diplomatic reaction to the campaign of the former American Senator D'Amato complement the picture of the Swiss nation's internally irritated sensibility.

All these aspects of political and public opinion reflecting a changing world explain why the revived debate at home and abroad regarding Switzerland's role, responsibility, accomplishments, and failures in World War II has affected the Swiss since 1995 with such lasting intensity. This is not because Switzerland, a few special issues and individual cases excepted, is confronted by newly discovered basic historical data. Quite to the contrary, it has to be stressed that since the 1950s the critical probing of the past has been pursued in impressive scholarship and with considerable public comment. Historical investigations and explanations are available particularly in those delicate areas where compromises were made and where success and failure often nearly collided. Obvious matters of political controversy remain, especially the refugee policy of a country encircled by Axis powers, the extent of aid Switzerland granted and refused, and manner of demarcation. This also applies to the monetary and gold policy of the Swiss National Bank. In an effort to secure the financial survival of the country it may have sometimes acted thoughtlessly in the purchase of looted gold from Axis-occupied countries; it may have gone too far in the procurement of internationally acceptable currency for the Nazi regime. To a somewhat lesser extent this also applies to the complex foreign trade relationships maintained by Switzerland during the war. Between blockade and counter-blockade of the two camps at war, the small country devoid of raw materials and wholly dependent on exports and imports had to secure adequate supplies for its people and its economic production by negotiating both with the Axis powers and with the Allies. Obviously the judgment about these trade relations, particularly those with Hitler's Germany, remains controversial. However, it is clear that the trade negotiations which Swiss delegates deftly and firmly conducted with both sides contributed significantly to the preservation of Swiss liberty and independence during the war years. The negotiators' achievement was that Switzerland could import more goods from Germany than it had to supply to it. On closer examination, the accusation raised in the Eizenstat report that Switzerland had indirectly contributed to the prolongation of the war cannot be sustained, as this last free country near Germany was in many respects most useful and helpful to the Allies.

Willing to Resist and Forced to Compromise

Among the various factors which restrained Hitler and Mussolini from occupying Switzerland was above all the ideological and political will to resist which animated most of the Swiss people and its political leadership. To this must be added the deterrent effect of the army which eventually was concentrated for defensive action in the mountains, the so-called redoubt. The foreign policy of neutrality also was decisive; its value was more clearly recognized and appreciated by the British Prime

Minister Winston Churchill than by the two large allied powers, the United States and the Soviet Union. Stuart Eizenstat's misplaced condemnation of Swiss neutrality misjudges its moral basis, the search for security. Neutrality in principle can certainly be combined with the requirements of an international order of peace. A scholarly inquiry by Professor Detlev F. Vagts published in the respected *American Journal of International Law* (and reproduced in this volume, Chapter VII) concludes that Switzerland during World War II acted in full conformity with then-current international rules.

One task of the international discussion consists of the need to explain and properly reconstruct the complex situation and the perils that a small and neutral country faced during the war years in a Hitler-controlled Europe. Those who were in active military service generally knew and still know that the country had to compromise in order to survive, even though these compromises were sometimes questionable. Having been spared from the ravages of war was certainly not simply paired with a white cloak of innocence. A myth of this type, which since the 1950s is perhaps more part of the foreign image of Switzerland than part of its self-image (which is itself not free of self-righteousness), has no justification. Where it still exists, it must be corrected by the current debate. Self-assertion in ruthless times is not child's play. The Fascist and National Socialist enemy threatened the country not only from the outside. Its fifth column, its sympathizers, and its adherents were also on the inside. This applies to the German-speaking part of the country as well as to the French and Italian-speaking regions. The University of Lausanne granted the Italian Duce and former "foreign worker" Mussolini in 1936 an honorary doctorate, an honor, however, which was not considered for Hitler, although in the early 1930s the "Front" movement in the German-speaking part of Switzerland appeared to be robust for a while and made itself felt in the early days of the war. After the defeat of France in 1940, the "Petition of the Two Hundred" was one of those (although unsuccessful) ventures that aimed at a political and journalistic adaptation of Switzerland to National Socialist ideology. During the threatening war times the small country also reacted to events out of fear. A thinly veiled anti-Semitism reflected in the behavior of certain officials, furthermore, is not a badge of honor either. In short: the struggle that had been waged between demands for compliant accommodation to the *Zeitgeist* of Hitler's Europe or for political and moral resistance was tough and hard-fought.

Survival as an Accomplishment

Has Switzerland, as some of its critics state, lived an historic lie by seeing itself after the war as having been a highly-threatened victim which, thanks to its dedication to heroic resistance and to its army, was able to protect and defend itself against Hitler, while in reality it was deliberately and knowingly spared by the Hitler regime as a useful collaborator in financial dealings and supply services? Much less accurate than the picture of the knight in shining armor is the image of Switzerland's purported wholesale and reprehensible adaptation and lack of character, as drawn by the historically uninformed former American Senator D'Amato and his many journalistic supporters. This also holds for the complaints and accusations coming out of New York in the international dispute about unclaimed accounts of Holocaust victims in Swiss banks. It remains a fact that the Swiss people and their government retained their political self-determination even during the years of Nazi totalitarianism. Among those elected to the House and Senate of the Swiss Parliament were at times only one or two who flirted with the idea of Switzerland's integration into a Hitler-dominated Europe. The Swiss press defended freedom and democracy against Germany's demands and totalitarianism. In the final analysis, the country did not throw itself into Hitler's arms, neither ideologically nor politically. It adhered to its tradition of neutrality in foreign policy (thus rejecting the opportunism advocated by Eizenstat) even after an Allied victory became a certainty and despite general popular opinion that morally supported vigorous resistance against Hitler. Herbert Lüthy, a renowned Swiss historian, assessed "the history of a possible collapse that did not take place" with keen insight: "The actual accomplishment of Switzerland during the 'time of Fascism'," he declared, "was *to survive*, without loss of inner substance and with maintenance of external independence: nothing more, nothing less."[2]

---

[2] Postscript to Georg Kreis, "July 1940. Operation Trump." In *The Thistles of 1940* (Basel 1973), 106; italics added.

Alternatives without a Chance

Was there a better alternative to the survival strategy of neutral Switzerland which would simultaneously have been both desirable and feasible? Internal self-surrender and renunciation of moral and political resistance, both of which the German propaganda machine tried its best to undermine, would also have weakened the effect of the army's deterrence and, as in Austria, eventually would have led to certain German occupation or annexation. Also a Swiss policy of rhetorical irritation and military provocation of the Hitler regime would have been nothing less than suicidal and, after the defeat of Belgium and France, would have led to an occupation of Switzerland by the Wehrmacht. This would have been true even after the somewhat changed conditions following the German defeat at Stalingrad in 1943, had the Swiss started to fight against Germany alongside the Allies. For Switzerland, encircled by Hitler's Germany and its allies, an assumption of Britain's role as pursued by Churchill was simply not an option. To enter the war on the side of the Allies after the American landing in Europe was incompatible with Swiss neutrality and, until shortly before the war's end, might still have led to a German occupation and destruction of the country. These and a subsequent liberation by the Allies would have served neither the Allies, the Swiss people, nor the roughly 300,000 refugees who had found a temporary haven in Switzerland; an occupation would simply have delivered the Swiss potential into German hands. In short, in spite of historical and political criticism, it is impossible to think of a convincing alternative to the survival strategy which Switzerland successfully pursued, even if at times at the cost of questionable compromises.

The successful survival strategy during World War II gave undamaged Switzerland a privileged position when the political and economic reconstruction of Europe began. Despite its outsider status as a neutral country and despite Allied criticism, Switzerland received at the end of the war respect and moral recognition that lasted for half a century. The end of the East-West conflict had provided neutral countries with a special political position and role between the blocs and had attributed to them a raison d'être outside of the bipolar divisions of the world powers; now neutral outsiders are forced at home and abroad to pursue critical self-examination and to gain renewed self-assurance.

It does not matter if the future of the country is seen today as full integration into Brussel's Europe or political autonomy outside of it. Yet the Swiss public is well served to deal seriously with the history of Switzerland during World War II. The coming generations as well as the gradually vanishing group of Swiss that had been actively engaged in the events of the war years, both need clear awareness of the merits and failures as well as reliable knowledge of the strengths and weaknesses of the nation's role in the Second World War. No one who lived through those times could then have been aware of all aspects involved, and scarcely a person born afterwards knows enough about those difficult times. Lights and shadows must be explored, and the public should know the full truth about the ruthless times of the war, about Hitlerism, and about the resistance against it.

The articles published in this volume deal with subjects that are central to the debate about the past. They offer not only factual historical information, but also contextual interpretations of the given controversial moral and political questions. They aim to contribute to a differentiated historical picture that withstands critical examination and serves as firm basis for an engaged dialogue about the past and the future.

PART ONE

ECONOMY

I: SWITZERLAND'S FOREIGN TRADE POLICY DURING WORLD WAR II:

Successful Perseverance of a Besieged Country

Hans Schaffner

That Switzerland was unexpectedly spared during World War II has from time to time been called a miracle. This view has genuine merit, particularly when one considers an old saying's claim that even miracles have to be earned. In any case, the Swiss people have not taken their being spared from war and foreign occupation, from hunger and misery, as a mere gift of fate or providence. Rather they did their utmost to keep danger from their borders and to make the miracle come to pass.

Oasis of Peace and Freedom

Switzerland fought hard but successfully to preserve its continued existence on four different levels. The first level was that of foreign policy: its goal was to present a clean balance sheet to foreign countries before the start of a threatening world conflict. The return to integral neutrality allowed Switzerland to assert itself as a neutral and democratic country even though it was located in the center of an Axis dominated and hostile Europe. Free from all one-sided alliances, the Swiss Confederation was able to escape joining a New Europe of a national-socialist hue, despite appeals that were never officially, but all the more unofficially made, and without causing open war with the Third Reich. We are probably still too close to the war years to fully acknowledge this achievement. In time, however, it will certainly be recognized as the creation of a foundation of foreign policy on which Switzerland was able to exist as an oasis of peace and freedom in the midst of a continent dominated by totalitarian regimes.

The second level of resistance centered on the military. It may be stated without exaggeration that Switzerland was one of the first countries to recognize the impending war and to draw the required

3

conclusions from this insight. The key words Vindonissa (demonstration of July 9, 1933 when demands were made for rearmament and better training of the army), Defense Bill (1934), Defense Loan (1936), Constitutional Proposal on the Development of the Country's Defense (1939) will probably be sufficient to remind readers of the planned precautionary measures to intensify Swiss defense readiness that were taken jointly by the authorities, the parliament, and the people. Only on the basis of these early preparations could the redoubt concept develop. At any rate, the Swiss army appeared to the Third Reich so well armed and so well led that an attack on Switzerland was postponed as too costly, until also the Swiss were finally liberated from Axis encirclement.

Emergency for the Wartime Economy

The third level of the Swiss endurance struggle in time of war was economic. While the Swiss army was fortunate to remain an "army in being", the wartime economy faced a bitter emergency. The guideline for this system, which perhaps may be best summarized by the terse formula "foresight, caring, work, and bread," could only be realized by thoughtful planning, guidance, and expanded cultivation. Maintaining a reasonable equilibrium between official organizations and private initiative contributed greatly to the success of those efforts. Contrary to a widely held opinion abroad, the Switzerland of World War II was no economic paradise nor a country of affluence; yet the efforts made by the wartime economy kept real hunger and real misery away from the country. All forms of unemployment were prevented, thereby social and political upheaval avoided.

The globally connected Swiss Confederacy was unable to take refuge in full self-sufficiency for even a few years. The greatest and best efforts of the domestic economy would have failed if Swiss authorities and Swiss commerce could not have maintained an exchange of goods with Switzerland's most important suppliers and markets despite all the obstacles created by blockade and counter-blockade. Considering that a double blockade ring encircled the country, this was not a matter of course. Maintaining import and export possibilities required also on the fourth level, that of trade policy, an extraordinary effort which entailed a real survival and endurance struggle.

The public, however, was least aware of this aspect as it was necessary to surround policy issues concerning foreign trade with a mantle of secrecy which was not less stringent than that of the military. This explains why it is still possible to meet Swiss today who believe that Switzerland provided for itself from its own soil, at least as far as food was concerned. The foreign trade statistics, however, which became again available to the public after the war, show that imported goods for 1940 to 1945 on average still amounted to half the size of the pre-war years. The averages for the years 1940 to 1943, when Switzerland was almost fully encircled by the Axis powers, disclose that imports of food and raw materials reached almost two-thirds of those in peacetime and almost three-quarters of the pre-war imports of manufactured goods. Such a volume of foreign trade was achieved primarily by the tenacious persistence and indefatigable efforts made by the Swiss negotiators of trade policy.

Pressure From Both Sides

There is hardly an aspect of the Swiss economy about which more falsehoods and misunderstandings have been spread in word and text as that of foreign trade. The milder of the accusations made during the war and still today is that Switzerland was forced into deals by the Axis powers; the harsher accusation is that it voluntarily supported the Axis war effort. The effort necessary to assure the provisioning of a small country is considered far too little by such critics, especially the level of effort required after the armed forces of the Western powers had left the continent at Dunkirk in the early summer of 1940 and Switzerland had become fully encircled by a hostile power. In a hard and tenacious struggle with both belligerents, it had to fight for every inch of living space. It is obvious that the most dramatic disputes erupted with the German Reich, which intended not only to cut off all imports, but also to use its formidable power to enforce its economic demands.

However, the Allied powers also did not refrain from pressure tactics against Switzerland so far as they were able to apply them. This occurred even at the start of the war. During the so-called "drôle de guerre", when people believed themselves to be safe behind the Maginot line, the Western powers wanted to subdue the enemy mainly by means of economic strangulation. In an attempt to close the blockade ring as tightly as possible, and in disregard of Switzerland's political and military neutrality, they asked the Swiss to suspend all trade with the German Reich and to align themselves with the Allied blockade.

Commerce In All Directions

Switzerland countered this request, which was beyond the limits of the possible, by insisting on the principle that it had to maintain foreign trade with all sides even in time of war; it also maintained as much as possible the given structure and scope of its commerce for reasons of neutrality as well as considerations of supply needs and the politics of exports. Switzerland also could not and would not accept any general obligations which would hinder the re-export of goods that had been processed within its territory. The Swiss Confederacy also claimed the right to freely trade the products of its domestic agriculture.

Extreme tenacity and patience were needed to get a hearing for this stance in Great Britain and France. Many obstacles had to be overcome, and it appeared many times that an understanding was impossible. Eventually on April 25, 1940 a blockade agreement was reached with France which satisfied the Swiss requirements to the extent that it permitted Swiss trade in all directions in principle and also did not unduly obstruct the exchange of goods with Germany. Switzerland was only prohibited from re-exporting goods in an unprocessed condition that had been imported from areas dominated by the Allies. After processing, re-export was permitted as usual, with few exceptions, even to enemy countries. This was a matter of great importance to Switzerland as an export-oriented industrial country. Most valuable also was that, based on some unpleasant experiences during World War One, Switzerland had already started before the war to establish a purely internal monitoring organization of foreign trade and was now able to make sure that the conditions set by the blockade powers concerning imports were strictly fulfilled. Switzerland rejected any foreign interference with this control mechanism or any other foreign actions aimed at control of it.

Encircled by the Axis Powers

The blockade agreement with the Allies was fully effective for only a short time. The military advance by the Third Reich against the West, which pushed the British armies out of the continent and forced France to capitulate, also presented Switzerland with a completely new situation. As an isolated country of four million in the midst of Axis-ruled Europe and treated with particular ill will by the German leadership as a "deserter from the Reich", the Swiss nation now entered the most dangerous phase of its history. Today, when it appears that a secure harbor has again been reached, it is not difficult to give advice about what should have been done differently or better during the years 1940 to 1944. What really counts is not a cheap know-it-all but an acknowledgment of the courage and determination of those people who helped lead the small country through the danger zone during those dark days when the German Reichsminister and SS-potentate Heinrich Himmler stood near Les Verrières in occupied France and, with a smirk on his face, peered into Switzerland. Apart from military preparedness and economic viability, now great circumspection in trade policy was needed to enable the Swiss nation to overcome the apparently hopeless situation.

In hindsight it is not hard to see the difficult situation Switzerland would have faced during the summer of 1940 if it had given in even an inch to the British-French demand to cut off trade relations with the German Reich. The steadfast adherence to the principles of neutrality and the universality of trade relations was vindicated. Referring to the previously negotiated blockade agreement with the Allies, in which one-sided commitments and associations that would have violated neutrality had been successfully avoided, Swiss negotiators were eventually able to reject a corresponding German demand to break off trade relations with Great Britain and the British Empire. This was certainly an important step; yet the actual resistance against German attempts to incorporate Switzerland into the economic potential of the Axis had just begun.

No Symmetrical Situation

It would have been impossible for the Swiss Confederation to roundly reject the German demands regarding the purchase of Swiss goods and the granting of Swiss clearing credits. It would have totally paralyzed Swiss economic life in a short time, or at best would have coldly strangled the country. Contrary to the situation in World War I, the economic pressures exerted on Switzerland by the two power groups were in no way equal or equally dangerous. Although the Allied blockade could exclude Swiss commerce from any supply and market areas overseas and thus inflict grievous damage, it was unable to suppress Swiss trade with the Axis powers, the Axis occupied regions, and the neutral countries of Europe. The Axis, in contrast, had the power and capability not only to cut off Switzerland from trade relations with the regions it controlled and with the neutral countries of Europe, but also to prevent acquisitions of supplies from overseas. This would have brought the whole Swiss economy to a standstill within a very short time and would have completely prevented the realization of the various military and economic defense plans as well as the crucial expansion of agricultural production. Under these circumstances Switzerland could not hope to maintain a balance between the two belligerent and blockading parties along the usual paths of trade policy as it had still been possible to a certain extent from 1914 to 1918, but had to think of new means and possibilities in order to fight off the Axis powers' economic encirclement.

Credit as a Weapon

This predicament readily explains the Swiss clearing credit policy which culminated in the granting of substantial credits to Germany. Besides the Swiss supply capability and the Swiss transport possibilities for the German-Italian transit traffic, these clearing advances were an important weapon in the hands of Swiss negotiators that allowed them to wrest sizable concessions from Germany. In this context, the individual phases of Swiss-German trade relations during World War II cannot be presented, but in hindsight it can be stated that, thanks to the use of Swiss economic and financial strength, it was possible not only to assure the supplying of Switzerland with coal, iron, lubricating oil, other indispensable industrial raw materials, and seeds and grains from the Axis countries, but to also maintain economic relations with the Allies.

Those from the Allied camp who view it as appropriate to repeatedly blame Switzerland for the scope of its trade with the Axis powers, tend to forget that Switzerland found itself in an extraordinarily precarious military and political situation. They also overlook the fact that Switzerland succeeded in attaining a substantial relaxation of the German counter-blockade in favor of the Allies. This reached the point at which Swiss industry exported important war materials, with German approval, through Axis-dominated territories to Great Britain and the United States. This represents a success of great and fundamental importance and confirms most convincingly that Switzerland was in this way preserving its sovereignty and neutrality during the time of Axis encirclement.

Daring Resistance

Even in peacetime the principle "do ut des" (which means that no service is performed without a partner's corresponding counter service) applies to the trade between nations. In wartime, this principle assumes even greater importance. Switzerland insisted throughout negotiations that economic relations with the Third Reich were always to occur within a framework of strict reciprocity. It gave the Germans only as much as was necessary in order not to conjure up a violent conflict. Swiss negotiators watched with eagle eyes so that each Swiss concession, be it the supply of goods, transit services, or clearing advances, was reciprocated by corresponding German concessions – that is, increased purchases of raw materials or increased export licenses for war-related goods to be sent to Allied countries. Switzerland did not hesitate for a moment to greatly reduce its shipments and credit services when German shipment capabilities started to drop off sharply after the first great defeat suffered by the German Wehrmacht during the Winter of 1942/43. To enforce its point of view, the Swiss Confederation did not shy away from repeatedly taking the risk of being without a treaty with Germany.

It should be noted that the first period of being without a treaty happened in early 1943 – exactly at a time when the Third Reich (as the Swiss intelligence service found out) again seriously contemplated a military invasion of Switzerland. However, Swiss negotiators and the

Swiss Federal Council did not abandon the chosen path of their trade policy even under pressure and threats. The negotiations between the Swiss and German delegates were tough and often stormy, but the Germans were never able to force Switzerland's capitulation with regard to trade policy, despite their occasional suspension of coal supplies or the announcement that the Hitler regime would repeal the immunity of Swiss ocean vessels and thus prevent vital food imports arriving from overseas.

Supplying Important War Goods

Although, as mentioned earlier, Swiss trade policy towards Germany in particular rested on the principle of service for equivalent service, in order to prevent misunderstandings it has to be pointed out that the value scale applied to the mutual exchange of goods greatly shifted due to realities of the war. This applies particularly to the Swiss point of view: before the war, and especially during times of crisis, imports were used in trade policy to achieve the greatest possible exports, but now the situation was such that, in reverse, exports were made to increase imports. It is quite obvious, however, that given the scarcity in war times, belligerent countries only supplied scarce raw materials to neutrals and non-allied countries if the non-belligerent nations supplied them in return with goods important to them. It is no surprise that those lifesaving goods which Germany required as compensation for coal, iron, and mineral oil were not abundant in Switzerland either. It was nevertheless considered preferable to export certain textiles, cattle, food (but never in substantial quantities) or electric power to Germany and to get in return basic goods important for survival and production, rather than to refuse the delivery of the requested manufactured goods and thereby bring the whole economy in a short time to a halt due to the lack of coal, iron and lubricants.

The other category of goods that was significant for Germany were items directly important to the war such as machine tools and precision instruments as well as actual war materials. Even in this category Switzerland was in no position to deny shipments unless it wanted to risk having Germany invoke trade policy reciprocity and thus exclude Switzerland from obtaining raw materials located in Germany and in

German-controlled areas, on the grounds that Switzerland had refused to cooperate.

More Imports than Exports

That Switzerland's behavior towards Germany was successful is particularly evident from the balance of trade resulting from the commerce between the two countries. German supplies of raw materials kept the Swiss economy working unimpeded for almost six years of the war's duration. As it became possible, due to German accommodation, to breach the counter-blockade and export important war goods to England and overseas destinations, the acquisition of food from Allied regions of influence was made easier in many ways. But it is especially important to note that between September 1, 1939 and April 30, 1945 Switzerland obtained from Germany goods valued at half a billion Swiss francs more than it supplied to it. Even if countries occupied by the German Wehrmacht such as Belgium, Holland and France are included, Switzerland still had an excess of imports over exports in the amount of 450 million francs. Thus in relation to German trade, Switzerland was the taking, not the giving, partner.

If the clearing traffic between Germany and Switzerland had to finance merely the export of Swiss goods, it would have been from the start not only fully self-supporting, but would have shown a surplus in favor of Switzerland. However, the financial traffic between the two nations had to take into account a number of other categories of claims (such as the transfer of profit from Swiss capital investments in Germany, payments relating to insurance and travel, payments for licenses, honoraria, etc.), which largely originated from the tight meshing of the Swiss and German economies before the war and before the National Socialists had come to power. As it was impossible to ignore these claims during the war, Switzerland had to grant Germany certain credit possibilities to meet these claims. It is therefore not devious to claim that the clearing advances of the Swiss government to the German Reich actually served the purpose of meeting financial obligations toward Germany that related to payments for items such as interest, insurance, and intellectual properties.

The Duties of Neutrality Were Met

It is also noteworthy to compare imports and exports which on the one hand occurred in the trade with the Axis powers and on the other in the commerce with the Allies. According to the calculations of the office of the Swiss Trade and Industry Association, the whole region under Axis domination, including the neutral countries of Europe which could be reached only through Axis controlled territory, supplied goods to Switzerland from the onset of the war to the end of 1944 in the amount of 7.1 billion Swiss francs and received from Switzerland goods in the amount of 5.3 billion francs. The fact that Switzerland imported more goods from the Axis powers than it exported to them makes the criticism that it supported mainly the war effort of the Axis particularly unjustified. Based on the calculations above, imports from the Allied countries during the war amounted to a value of 2 billion Swiss francs, while the exports to these countries were only 1.7 billion francs. Since Switzerland had been totally within the sphere of the German counter-blockade from June 1940 until August 1944, this should be rated as quite a success. It is proof that Switzerland – given all the unfavorable circumstances of the times and the power arrangements it had to consider – never swerved from the path assigned to it by the duties of a free, independent and neutral country.

Counterproductive Reaction of the Allies

Switzerland's efforts to maintain its sovereignty, neutrality and economic power in midst of an Axis-dominated continent did not always find full understanding and support in the Allied camp. The trade agreement of August 9, 1940 between Switzerland and Germany which contained the ground rules for the wartime accounting between the two countries and for the clearing regulations was certainly not well received by the Allies. The Allied blockade authorities tightened the guidelines for provisioning Switzerland; the country had to manage almost completely without industrial raw materials from the Allied sphere of influence (only fats for soap production and certain raw materials for purely military purposes were granted to Switzerland in very restricted quantities), the supply of food was greatly reduced, and at times the issuance of navicerts (shipping documents) for the importation of overseas commodities was even totally stopped.

These measures were always cited in context with Swiss services to Germany and in part also to Italy, be it the delivery of goods or clearing advances. However, if the British and – after the United States of America entered the war – other Anglo-Saxon authorities concerned with economic warfare and blockade also were hoping that Switzerland could be coerced by import restrictions and other pressure meant to reduce its goods traffic with the Axis powers, the appropriateness of the methods they employed had to be questioned from the start. The fact that Switzerland could not obtain raw materials from Allied areas forced Switzerland to grant the German Reich added concessions for the sole purpose of getting deliveries of raw materials which were not obtainable from the Allied camp. Thus the tightening of the Allied blockade intensified commerce between Switzerland and its neighbor to the north instead of diminishing it. Allied measures forced Switzerland artificially into an even greater economic dependency on the Axis powers, which controlled the continent and already had militarily encircled the country.

The Usefulness of the Defense

It must be stressed that Switzerland also later opposed those Allied demands which it viewed as incompatible with its sovereignty or neutrality in the same decisive manner as it had rejected German impositions. Thus in 1943 the Americans and the British threatened certain Swiss companies with blacklisting and with exclusion from trade with the Allies even after the war. Via the British and American embassies they hoped to force those Swiss firms to accept conditions according to which they would have totally ceased or substantially reduced their exports to Germany. The Federal Council fought such an intrusion by the Western powers into Swiss trade relations with other nations and on November 4, 1943 prohibited companies from entering into any obligations with foreign embassies concerning commerce with foreign countries.

Switzerland's foreign trade policy greatly contributed to the safeguarding of its economic strength, sovereignty, and independence during World War II. As sufficient importation of food and raw materials formed an important basis for strengthening of military defense readiness, efforts in the area of foreign trade also contributed directly to the maintenance of armed neutrality. The conclusion of the Currie agreement showed that the Swiss efforts eventually were not completely ignored by the Allies despite their complaints; after a painful interruption of almost a year the agreement reopened the economic gates to the West on March 7, 1945 and renewed Switzerland's trade relations with the Western Allies.

More than Self-Interest

On the basis of the data above, we have endeavored to help clarify those misunderstandings which often have stood in the way of a just assessment of Swiss trade policy during World War II. These misunderstandings have been harmful to Switzerland's image abroad as well as to its internal peace. Hopefully the above has shown that by its trade policy Switzerland had asserted itself in a hard, painful, and extremely dangerous struggle with the Axis powers. Another aspect which has been somewhat shortchanged in discussions on Swiss trade policy needs to be mentioned. When Switzerland was able to keep from its borders war, occupation, hunger, and misery in a fourfold endurance struggle for its existence, it rendered a service not only to itself, but unquestionably also to the future rebuilding of Europe. In view of the terrible material and moral damage suffered by the continent, any part of its soil over which the banner of freedom was never furled and the economic structure remained unbroken has gained particular importance.

After the war, Switzerland's financial strength greatly contributed to the economic recovery of Europe and its undamaged industrial system benefitted several European nations. These facts are stressed not as cheap self-praise but because it is time to understand at home and abroad that Switzerland's hard resistance against those in power in the Third Reich was not just a Swiss issue, but also a European issue.

If one considers the given circumstances, Switzerland may rightfully claim to have done everything possible for the cause of freedom in its domain. If it had been attacked by Germany it would have defended itself to the utmost; as it was spared this fate, it defended its independence – as a neutral and non-belligerent nation – with all available means, not least those of its trade policy. For this, the responsible leaders of Swiss trade policy during World War II deserve the gratitude of the Swiss people.

II: NEUTRALITY AND ECONOMIC WARFARE

Klaus Urner

Although Switzerland was almost completely spared direct military engagements, it still had to fight offensively for economic survival. Despite its declared neutrality, it had to face economic warfare on two fronts, which endangered its very existence because of its great dependence on foreign trade. Along with Belgium and the Netherlands, the Swiss Confederation was among the countries with the highest per capita foreign trade, which highlights Switzerland's tight involvement in the world economy. More than half of its 4.2 million inhabitants were working in, and sustained by, the export sector. Because the country lacked substantial mineral resources, it had to import the raw materials which were processed into semi-finished and finished goods. Before the war, people assumed that the food produced domestically would cover the caloric needs of the Swiss for just about six months.[1]

Switzerland's dependence on transport routes also further revealed its precarious position in the event of a world-wide conflict. It had, furthermore, no sea ports and had to rely for imports and exports on the consent of its neighbors. It sought to meet disturbances in global commerce by widely spread trade agreements which, however, were largely concentrated in Europe. Having learnt from mistakes made during World War I, Switzerland developed over time an efficient wartime economic organization which contributed decisively to the prevention of hunger and mass unemployment.[2]

---

[1] *4 Jahre wirtschaftliche Landesverteidigung.* 2. Auflage. Schriftenreihe des Aufklärungs-dienstes der Eidgenössischen Zentralstelle für Kriegswirtschaft (Bern 1943), 28-29.

[2] Hans Schaffner, "Eidgenössische Zentralstelle für Kriegswirtschaft," in: *Die schweizerische Kriegswirtschaft 1939/1948. Bericht des eidgenössischen Volkswirtschafts-Departementes.* (Bern 1950), 1-52. The official publication contains a plethora of material and statistics pertaining to the whole wartime economy. Cited from here on as *Kriegswirtschaft.* Hermann Böschenstein, *Bundesrat Obrecht 1882-1940* (Solothurn 1981), 241ss; Klaus Urner, "Une

Despite efforts such as intensive farming methods, the use of substitute materials, systematic recycling, and far-sighted stockpiling, it was impossible to retreat into self-sufficiency. Economic pressures from the Axis powers as well as from the Allies threatened Switzerland's very existence, and Switzerland's foreign trade policy faced the difficult task of preventing its being strangled by blockade and counter-blockade. That Switzerland procured successfully, although with occasional interruptions, life-saving supplies in sufficient quantities to permit a relatively comfortable survival in the midst of a suffering Europe proves the success of this trade policy. It remains, however, controversial to this day, mainly because of the means used to secure such favorable economic conditions.

The criticism particularly targets Switzerland's supply of war materials and the Federal Government's granting credits, which by June 1940, substantially benefited the Axis powers. By the time the Third Reich capitulated, Switzerland's advances granted in the clearing traffic with Germany and its occupied areas amounted to 1,119 million Swiss francs. To this must be added debts in the trade with Italy, which inclusive of private debts amounted to about 380 million francs. The liquidation agreement concluded with the Federal Republic of Germany on August 26, 1952 yielded a repayment of merely 650 million francs, of which 250 million were reinvested in that neighboring country.[3] Yet weighing more heavily than the financial losses was Switzerland's broad international isolation after the war; its neutrality was by then viewed with suspicion. Many at home and abroad falsely accused the country of having primarily supported the Axis powers in violation of its neutrality by exports of important armaments and especially by financing these exports with generous credits. There was a malicious saying that the Swiss worked for six days of the week for the Axis and then prayed for an Allied victory on the seventh.

---

mobilisation pour les besoins de l'Économie de guerre" in: *Revue d'histoire de la deuxième guerre mondiale*, no. 121 (January 1981), 63-69.

[3] *Kriegswirtschaft*, 83ss, 107. "Die schweizerisch-deutschen Finanazabkommen," *Neue Zürcher Zeitung,* No. 2813, December 11, 1952; "Die Investitionen des Bundes aus der 'Clearingmilliarde' in Westdeutschland,".ibid., No. 2006, September. 2, 1953. A settlement of private claims was reached by the agreement of. October 12, 1956; see *Bundesblatt* (Bern 1956), 429ss.

As the actual situation is difficult to understand, such attacks have an easy time. But first an evaluation is necessary to clarify how far the economic sector can legitimately be made the touchstone of Swiss neutrality. In an effort to present a positive view of the conduct of foreign trade policy, the side opposing the critics insists that neutrality was scrupulously observed in all trade negotiations. Some important facts have been marshaled to counter the reproach of one-sided shipments. For one, in its trade with the Axis powers Switzerland gained a significant surplus of imports over exports in value as well as in quantity. Just in the exchange of goods with Germany (which became increasingly unable to cover its own needs due to the expansion of the war), Switzerland succeeded in getting considerably more provisions into Switzerland than it had to supply in exports to Germany, to the tune of about half a billion Swiss francs. Even the trade with overseas countries and the Allies was in no way insubstantial; goods valued at about 1.7 billion francs were exported through the double blockade; imports amounted to two billion francs, which was about a third of the trade volume reached with the Axis powers.[4] These summary data already provide a more differentiated and complex picture than Switzerland's critics admit. However, the question regarding credits and war materials remains unanswered or, as in the official accounting report of 1950, is treated in an obviously one-sided manner. Yet interpretations which simply view the credit granted by the Swiss Government to the Axis as a consequence of an otherwise advantageous agreement that also allowed the inclusion of the so-called invisibles into the clearing exchange (items such as interest and dividends from Swiss capital exports to Germany and also payments for insurance, travel, licenses, administration, and honoraria), remain questionable. Switzerland was neither able nor willing to renounce these claim categories for this difficult debtor, justly so when one remembers that the Swiss credit balance in Germany at the end of 1932 had amounted to about 2.7

---

[4] Data differ, depending on the system of calculation and whether occupied areas are included; *Kriegswirtschaft*, 64-65, 82; Heinrich Homberger, *Schweizerische Handelspolitik im Zweiten Weltkrieg. Ein Überblick auf Grund persönlicher Erlebnisse.* (Erlenbach-Zürich 1970), 116; Ernst Speiser, "Die schweizerisch-deutschen Handelsbeziehungen während des Krieges" in *Schweizer Monatshefte,* 12 (März 1946), 745-746.

billion Reichsmark.[5] As German deliveries of goods exceeded the value
of Swiss exports, one might conclude in a purely mathematical sense
that no credit would have been necessary without including the
invisibles. Such an attempt to keep the financial advances made by
Switzerland to Germany out of any problematic context fails in view of
the structure which formed the basis of the agreements. Not only were
there different kinds of credit, but all Swiss economic relations with
Germany became dependent on financial advances.[6] Separation of credit
from trade at a later date is impossible.

A one-sided calculation has also been applied to the controversial
exports of war materials. An illustrative example is attributed to
National Councilor Ernst Speiser, the head of the War Industry and
Labor Office. He estimated the total value of exports to Germany during
the war at about 2.5 billion francs and assumed an annual average of 443
million Swiss francs. Speiser then calculated that, depending on the type
of goods, 40,000 to 60,000 workers were needed in order to produce the
value of these exports. He concluded that, given Switzerland's approximately two million working people, a maximum of three percent
"worked for Germany".[7]

This approach, however, gives an equally undifferentiated answer
to wholesale criticism. Neither the special position of war-related
exports nor their overwhelming importance in the overall agreement
concluded with Germany is considered. The accusation of partisanship,
furthermore, specifically targeted those branches of production occupied
with the manufacture of weapons, ammunition, ball bearings, ignitions,
machine tools, precision instruments, and other goods indispensable to
the war effort. Did Swiss foreign trade policy thereby pursue a path that
was incompatible with neutrality? This question is of particular interest
in this context, but it cannot be investigated without considering the
possibilities and limitations of economic survival. From a larger

---

[5] Eugen Roesle, *Die Finanzforderung im schweizerisch-deutschen Verrechnun-
gsverkehr* (Basel, 1944), 2-3. In 1932 100 Reichsmark equaled 123.457 francs.

[6] See *Kriegswirtschaft*, 82, from which the official interpretation derives which
sees the credits judged solely in connection with the invisibles. Homberger,
Schweizerische Handelspolitik, 48ff., interprets the function of the clearing credits
with greater differentiation.

[7] Speiser, "Handelsbeziehungen," 47.

perspective, a comparison with Sweden in particular provides a more reliable view of the issues raised by blockade warfare which ignored previously made agreements and which neutral countries could only solve in a pragmatic manner. A comprehensive treatise on Swiss foreign trade relations during the war years is lacking, but it is possible to use relevant publications that explore overall developments as well as individual issues.[8]

Trade Policy as a Survival Strategy for Switzerland and Sweden: The Limitations of Comparison

To start from the overall context which also provides the real framework for the question of economic neutrality, it is worthwhile to compare how economic warfare changed the foreign trade of Switzerland and Sweden. Both countries shared the common goal of reducing their dangerous dependence on Germany and, if possible, overcoming it. Sweden became economically dependent by the German occupation of Denmark and Norway in April 1940, and Switzerland shortly thereafter by the defeat of France. The analogies in their development are numerous and can even be detected in the similar changes in their birth and death rates.[9] Seen from the outside, the parallels are quite obvious; both countries were neutral and remained islands of peace in a Europe beset by war. The means at their disposal to maintain their economic independence, however, were not identical. This difference is particularly relevant for judging the foreign trade policy each pursued, even without assessing whether Switzerland or Sweden initially faced a relatively more favorable position in regard to the blockades.

Even before the war Sweden covered 91 percent of its food requirements by its own agriculture, while Switzerland with only 52 percent self-sufficiency in food was more vulnerable to attempts at

---

[8] See the references in the articles of Heinz K. Meier, D. Bourgois, and K. Urner in the section "Economie et neutralité" in: *Revue d'histoire de la deuxième guerre mondiale*, no. 121 (Janvier 1981), 35-69.

[9] Bank Internationalen Zahlungsausgleich (BIZ), *14. Jahresbericht* (Basel, 1944), 10, 18.

extortion.[10] The danger of starvation was countered with the well-conceived "Wahlen Plan", the so-called cultivation battle, but even the doubling of cultivation in Switzerland by 1944 did not grant complete independence.[11] In contrast to Switzerland, which has few raw materials, Sweden had valuable mineral resources; besides nonferrous and precious metal ores, these included primarily excellent iron ores. These facts served as an effective argument during trade negotiations with Germany. During World War II, Swedish exports provided for more than a quarter of German iron ore supplies and were thus of prime economic importance to the Third Reich's war effort.[12] In contrast, Switzerland did not possess supplies which because of their desirability were quite as effective assets, yet during negotiations Swiss officials could bring up the advantages of transit and also the important element of the capital strength of the national and private economy. The gold and currency reserves of the Swiss National Bank in 1940-41 were double those of the Swedish National Bank, and the comparatively small increase of Swiss bank note circulation indicates that in 1939 considerable liquid assets existed.[13]

Due to these different circumstances, Switzerland was forced and able to provide greater financial services than Sweden to secure its imports. Because of varying market conditions dictated by a wartime economy, price levels for German goods were lower in Sweden than in Switzerland, at least towards the end of the war. If necessary, the Third

---

[10] BIZ, *15. Jahresbericht* (Basel 1945), 50.

[11] Friedrich T. Wahlen, "Das schweizerische Anbauwerk im Zweiten Weltkrieg," in: *Innen- und Aussenpolitik: Primat oder Interdependenz? Festschrift zum 60. Geburtstag von Walther Hofer*, edited by Urs Altermatt and J. Garamvölgyi (Bern 1980), 353-365. Switzerland was able to avoid the rationing of potatoes and vegetables. Ernst Feisst, "Eidgenössisches Kriegs-Ernährungsamt," in *Kriegswirtschaft*, 157-188.

[12] Klaus Wittmann, *Schwedens Wirtschaftsbeziehungen zum Dritten Reich 1933-1945* (München 1978), 243, 396. The controversial question raised in the studies of Rolf Karbom, Alan S. Milward and Jörg-Johannes Jäger as to whether Germany would have been able to conduct a world war at all without Swedish iron ore shows the importance of these shipments, yet it is impossible to raise the question in such an absolute form.

[13] BIZ, *11. Jahresbericht* (Basel 1941), 153ff; *15. Jahresbericht* (Basel 1945), 73.

Reich could make do without trade with Switzerland, especially since Germany itself urgently needed the iron and coal it exported to that country, while the need for Swedish raw materials kept on rising. The increased demand for steel of high quality made Sweden's low phosphorus ore particularly desirable. Only if one overlooks these divergent conditions is it possible to reach the wrong conclusion that, in contrast to Switzerland, Sweden's ability to terminate its trade with Germany without a credit balance permits by itself a fair assessment of the foreign trade policy pursued by the two countries.

The statement that Germany had fully met its supply obligations towards Sweden must be accompanied by the reason for this remarkable German response.[14] During the phase of its decline, the Third Reich did not keep its agreements with Switzerland because neither Swiss credits nor the production of important war-related items had achieved a sufficient level of priority to compel Germany to fulfill its contractual obligations. Thus Switzerland's options for negotiation were far narrower than Sweden's. The Swiss Confederation's primary goal was not the clearing balance, but the securing of provisions which credits made possible.[15] That Swiss exports of war material did not have the same priority as the Swedish delivery of iron ore is documented by the remarkable fact that until around 1940 Germany saw no need to make demands on the Swiss armament industry. Only after the armistice with France did Germany strive to exploit all available production potential. It assumed that the small countries of Europe had no choice but to join the new continental economy directed from Berlin and Rome.[16] Switzerland as well as Sweden (which now exported ball bearings

---

[14]Wittmann, *Schwedens Wirtschaftsbeziehungen*, 391. The claim that Stockholm committed under Allied pressure a breach of contract with Germany is raised by Swedish authors Gunnar Hagglöf, *Svensk Krigshandelspolitik under andra världskriget* (Stockholm 1958), 282, and Wilhelm Carlgren, *Svensk Utrikespolitik 1939-45* (Stockholm 1973), 545.

[15] See statistics for the import and export balance between Germany and Switzerland in *Kriegswirtschaft*, 80-81; also in *Statistisches Jahrbuch der Schweiz 1949* (Basel 1950), 292ff, 306ff.

[16] The German propaganda publication *Um die Neugestaltung der europäischen Wirtschaft. Deutsche Prominente sprechen* (1941), contains a collection of related statements. See also Walter Funk, "Wirtschaftliche Neuordnung Europas!" Reprint from: *Südost-Echo*, July 26, 1940.

mostly to the German sphere of influence) were forced by the counter-blockade to make a complete reversal in their foreign trade policy.

The actual importance of Swiss war-related exports to the Axis powers has been, in retrospect, overrated. These exports were vital for Switzerland, not for the Reich. Lacking other possibilities, the exports provided the Swiss an advantage in negotiations besides considerations such as allowing an unimpeded currency and gold trade or even the use of the Gotthard transit route. These were equal factors in the overall context, but could not be applied flexibly in negotiations because of the difficulty of calculating their efficacy. But Swiss war-related exports were sufficiently desired to induce Germany to make important concessions concerning imports and to allow a certain permeability of the counter-blockade. The German chief negotiator, Ministerial Counsel Seyboth, highlighted this fact when he evaluated the agreement of February 7, 1941 as follows:

> I think that I agree with Mr. Hemmen that a concession to Switzer-land regarding the continued supply of coal and iron cannot be avoided. If Switzerland supplies us now to such an extent with most important war materials one may not maintain anymore that Switzer-land is unimportant for us as a supply country and thus should be placed behind other countries for receiving coal and iron.[17]

Although this illustrates the significance of war-related exports in the context of negotiations, it also immediately reveals the implied limited Swiss ability to wrest concessions from Germany that were diametrically opposed to Germany's interests. Particularly in the numerous attempts to restart trade with the Allies and to supply them as well with important war-related goods, the Swiss negotiators found themselves on slippery ground. In June 1943, after months of acute

---

[17] Circular of Feb. 21, 1941, signed Sabath. *Akten betreffend Schweiz*, Vol. 8 (January 1940 – August, 1942), HaPol, AA (Handelspolitische Abteilung, AA) Politisches Archiv des auswärtigen Amtes, Bonn (PA-B). Johannes Richard Hemmen was head of the economics section of the German embassy in Bern with the rank of ambassador; in June 1940 he was also influential in the armistice commission which met in Wiesbaden regarding economic issues. He proved to be an arrogant chief agent and was replaced in 1943; see Homberger, *Schweizerische Handelspolitik*, 92.

tensions in trade relations with Germany, German Secretary of State Steengracht stated to Swiss Minister Fröhlicher that

> If Switzerland absolutely insists on dissolving economic relations with Germany, that will not be an important problem for Germany. All of the German orders placed in Switzerland are only a fraction of one percent of the German armament capacity. We will win the war just as well with or without the increase of the production by this fraction of a percent. Switzerland will be the only one to suffer.

The Swiss Confederation, however, still persisted in its efforts to reduce exports of war materials to Germany because Germany no longer fulfilled its obligations. Yet the Reich also did not want to forego the advantages of relations with an economy that had been spared destruction. The art of negotiating consisted in expanding the Swiss freedom of movement as far as possible without going too far. A temporary halt to Swiss coal imports or interruptions in negotiations was tolerable, but the systematic starving of the Swiss people that could result from total confrontation had to be avoided.

The institution of clearing exchanges and a state-controlled war economy permitted the basic principle 'do ut des' [give so that you get] of foreign trade to be applied with unrelenting consistency. Even before the war's start, about one-third of Swiss foreign trade occurred via clearing operations, and by 1942 this share had increased to about three-quarters. Within Europe, payments could be made freely only with Sweden and Portugal.

Effects of the Counter-blockade on the Geographic
Restructuring of Foreign Trade

The total of Switzerland's imports and exports increased in value until the turn of the year 1942, but after the start of the war the imports shrank rapidly in quantity; in 1942 this was only about half and in 1944 not even a third of the prewar year 1939. Additionally, the size of exports was much reduced after 1941. This diverging development reflects an enormous increase in the price of imports. Between June 1939 and June 1944, wholesale prices increased in Switzerland by 110 percent, in Sweden by 81 percent, while the cost of living rose by 52 and

42 percent respectively.[18] At the end of 1942 both countries were able to control price increases by having stable currencies, yet Switzerland had to take into account the high costs of goods from overseas, among them principally food and animal feed. A further aspect that influenced foreign trade policy was the difference in geopolitical position which, due to the distortions of economic warfare, did not always lead to predictable results.

During World War II Sweden had a commercial fleet of more than 1,200 steam and motor vessels with a total capacity of almost one million gross register tons (BRT).[19] Its efficient ports were excellently equipped for overseas trade, so that the German blockade of the Skagerrak hit Sweden all the more seriously. Its large-scale loss of extensive markets outside of continental Europe made it easier for Germany to force itself on Sweden as its absolutely pre-eminent trading partner. Sweden could not exploit the expected advantage of its commercial fleet, although it benefited from it in the so-called "Gothenburg traffic", that is, the opening to the West that depended on Germany. Switzerland, in contrast, depended not only on transit permits through both blockades, but also on the use of the technical installations of foreign countries. Genoa, Barcelona, Lisbon, and later Marseilles were its main transshipment ports.

Securing the necessary space on vessels implied numerous difficulties. After the war in the Balkans, the fifteen Greek ships chartered by Switzerland were no longer permitted to dock in Italian ports, and in early 1941 five of them even had to be ceded to England. The Swiss Federal Council decided on April 9, 1941 henceforth to permit deep-sea shipping under the Swiss flag, which previously had been avoided because of the danger of becoming involved in international conflicts. The Swiss Confederation itself bought four ships with a capacity of 27,230 tons, to which were added several freighters from Swiss shipping lines and eight charter vessels with a total loading capacity of more than

---

[18] B.R. Mitchell, *European Historical Statistics 1750-1970* (London 1976), pp. 497, 746; *Statistisches Jahrbuch der Schweiz 1949*, pp. 281, 545; BIZ, *14th Annual Report* (Basel 1944), pp. 50ss, 87-88.

[19] Mitchell, ibid., p. 630.

100,000 tons.[20] Thus, some bottlenecks excepted, lack of transport possibilities did not diminish shipments from overseas. The handicap of not being a nation with seafaring experience was solved so effectively that at times more shipping space than needed was available. Most obstacles were encountered in the handling of the blockade and in problems of transshipment in the ports.

The following table shows the dramatic shifts that economic warfare forced on the foreign trade of both countries:

Foreign Trade with Belligerent Countries
Switzerland vs. Sweden[21]

Switzerland's Imports	(Percent of Total Imports)						
	1938	1939	1940	1941	1942	1943	1944
From: Germany & Austria	25	23	23	32	32	31	37
Italy	7	7	9	12	8	8	2
France	14	15	8	4	4	5	4
Great Britain	6	6	5	1	1	*	*
United States	8	7	11	8	12	3	2

Sweden's Imports	(Percent of Total Imports)						
From: Germany & Austria	24	26	40	54	47	51	49
Italy	n/a	2	n/a	8	7	4	n/a
France	3	3	1	1	*	1	*
Great Britain	18	18	9	1	1	1	1
United States	16	17	16	8	5	3	3

---

[20] *Kriegswirtschaft*, pp. 110-146. Regarding the problem of ocean shipping and neutrality see "Sind Schiffe unter Schweizerflagge Bestandteil des schweizerischen Territoriums?" *Neue Zürcher Zeitung*, III, No. 1285 (August 14, 1942).

[21] Calculations based on data in Mitchell, ibid., 497, 566ff.; *Statistisches Jahrbuch der Schweiz 1949*, 281, 290-291, 304-305; *Bericht über Handel und Industrie der Schweiz im Jahre 1944*, published by the Vorort des Schweizerischen Handels-und Industrie-Vereins (Zürich 1945), 33ff.; *Kriegswirtschaft*, 65. The information in Wittmann, *Schwedens Wirtschaftsbeziehungen*, 404-405 is based on incomplete numbers from the year 1944 and is used here only for the data on trade between Sweden and Italy.

Switzerland's Exports (Percent of Total Exports)

	1938	1939	1940	1941	1942	1943	1944
To: Germany & Austria	19	15	22	39	42	37	26
Italy	7	6	11	13	10	6	*
France	9	11	9	6	4	3	2
Great Britain	11	13	7	2	1	2	3
United States	7	10	11	7	7	9	13

Sweden's Exports (Percent of Total Exports)

	1938	1939	1940	1941	1942	1943	1944
To: Germany & Austria	18	20	37	43	42	47	41
Italy	n/a	2	n/a	7	9	4	n/a
France	3	3	1	1	1	1	*
Great Britain	25	23	9	2	2	*	1
United States	9	10	4	1	2	*	*

Note: * = Less than one percent

These foreign trade statistics provide a different overall picture than most researchers have imagined, one that is considerably more favorable to Switzerland than to Sweden. While Switzerland was able to strengthen its traditionally solid European connections, at times it had to face the dominance claimed by the Third Reich. In 1938 the imports from Germany had amounted to a quarter of the total value of all imports. From 1941 to 1944 this share was around one third and thus was clearly lower than the Swedish one. In 1942 exports to Germany from both neutral countries were at the same level, but after that date Switzerland reduced them drastically. However, here too one must consider the interdependence deriving from geographic location and the efficacy of the double blockade.

Although it viewed itself as only a temporarily-spared island in the center of the Axis sea under constant threat of being totally cut off, Switzerland used its economic advantages derived from geographic location even under these difficult circumstances. While Sweden faced only the single negotiating partner Germany who had sole control over the counter-blockade, Switzerland was able to take advantage of certain differences in the handling of the blockade by Italy, its southern neighbor. Although Italy tried to exploit Switzerland's predicament with excessive prices and credit demands, it nevertheless remained in comparison the more manageable Axis partner. In particular, the transit agreement concluded on November 4, 1939, which guaranteed free transit of goods through Italy, proved most valuable so long as Italian authorities were in charge, despite the painful obstructions of the coordinated counter-blockade. Vichy France could not circumvent the blockade; Germany had seen to that. According to the German-French armistice agreement, its ports could not be used for transshipment. While in 1942 Switzerland sent only 405 empty railroad cars to France for the importation of goods, this number increased to 16,579 despite the 1943 occupation of Vichy by German troops.[22] After Italy's capitulation in September 1943, its ports were no longer available, but Marseilles could now be utilized. After the total encirclement by Germany, Switzerland lost all imports because of the increased Allied blockade, and imports dropped in 1944 to the lowest level since 1888. When Italy left the Axis, Germany was already weakened in its negotiating position towards Switzerland by the deterioration of its power, and had to moderate its aggressive tone.

While considerably intensifying their mutual trade, both neutral countries, Sweden and Switzerland, tried to find substitute markets after the 1940 collapse of commerce with Great Britain, France, and Belgium.[23] The remaining possibilities were generally the same, except that Sweden was less successful because of its marginal position in continental Europe, which made the German blockade most efficient. In contrast, Slovakia, Hungary, Romania, and Turkey as well as Spain and Portugal provided Switzerland with food and raw materials. The Allies were not able to interfere directly in trade relations within the European continent but did control all overseas traffic with their blockade ring. As long as the United States remained neutral, it was possible to maintain at least the value of trade above that of 1938, and in 1942 wheat imports still reached Switzerland in a record amount of 163.1 million francs. After that, the United States proved to be even more unyielding than Great Britain, so that overseas trade relations were instead intensified with countries such as Argentina, Cuba, and Brazil in the interest of promoting import shipments.

---

[22] *Kriegswirtschaft*, 102, 133-134.

[23] Regarding the relationship between Sweden and Switzerland see the article by Marco Durrer in *Schwedische und schweizerische Neutralität im Zweiten Weltkrieg* (1985), 155ff; Hans Rudolf Briner, *Die Wirtschaftsbeziehungen Schweiz-Skandinavien*, Dissertation Zürich. Zürich 1970, 181ff.

Although commerce with Great Britain shrank to a minimum, in contrast to most of its other trade relations, Switzerland had always shipped more goods, measured by value, to the British than it received. This also applied to the critical phase of 1943-44 when the Allies withheld urgently needed imports from Switzerland in order to force an accelerated reduction of trade with Germany.[24] The country was poorly rewarded for its efforts to overcome the counter-blockade. The result is all the more impressive and the comparison speaks for itself. (Values for Sweden are added in its currency, which was then slightly stronger.)

In 1943, Swiss exports to Great Britain were still 35.7 million Swiss francs, those of Sweden 2 million Swedish kronor. British imports to Switzerland amounted only to 3.6 million Swiss francs, yet those to Sweden 15 million Swedish kronor. In the following year, British goods valued at 1.2 million Swiss francs reached Switzerland, while those sent to Sweden were valued at 16 million Swedish kronor. Switzerland shipped goods to Great Britain for 34 million Swiss francs, Sweden for 6 million Swedish kronor. The disproportion in the trade with the USA was also staggering. In 1943 Switzerland shipped goods – among them were more and more products indispensable to the war effort – through the counter-blockade to the United States for about 153 million Swiss francs, Sweden for 1 million Swedish kronor; yet the USA had curtailed its shipments to Switzerland to less than a quarter of the value of the preceding year, that is to 56.4 million Swiss francs compared to 60 million Swedish kronor for Sweden. The following year Switzerland obtained only 21.2 million Swiss francs worth of goods from North America, and Sweden 2 million kronor, while the exports amounted to 140.8 million Swiss francs, those of Sweden 2 million Swedish kronor. This excess of exports to imports, welcome in peacetime, had at that time a totally opposite significance because during that period the main goal of exports was to secure imports. While in 1944 Sweden still supplied goods to Germany amounting to 349 million kronor, but

---

[24] Cassian Hobi, *Die Wirtschaftsbeziehungen Schweiz-Grossbritannien.* Dissertation Zürich, (Mels 1959), 115ff.

channeled goods to Great Britain and the USA for only 8 million kronor, the ratio for Switzerland was 294 to 175 million Swiss francs![25]

These very clear results must be weighed in the examination of certain claims, however, so that the limits of comparison also become clear. A reasoned evaluation is not possible by simply presenting a synoptic analysis, but only by a consideration of the specific circumstances of both nations. The ability and tenacity of the respective negotiating delegations are to be measured by the extent of their success in realizing their goals of national self-preservation in the economic war in light of the different conditions they faced and in conformity with the two countries' perception of neutrality.

The Conduct of Economic Neutrality

Each belligerent party pursued a double goal with its blockade policy towards the neutral countries: on the one hand it aimed to prevent the enemy benefitting from the goods shipped, and on the other it was merely a question of power to make the whole economic potential dependent on one's own side and to one's own advantage. During World War I Switzerland had not been sufficiently savvy at defending itself from the resulting dangers. For monitoring foreign trade, surveillance organizations were created which were based on concepts of private law although they largely performed public duties. This setup was supposed to protect the independence of the official agencies towards the outside, but in fact promoted just the opposite. The Société Suisse de Surveillance Économique [Swiss Association for Economic Surveillance], established in the fall of 1915, succumbed to the dictates of the Entente without the Swiss government being able to suppress their direct intervention into domestic economic life. The Central Powers tried too late to pull even by using the Schweizerische Treuhandstelle für die

---

[25] Mitchell, 567, 569; *Statistisches Jahrbuch der Schweiz 1949*, 290-291., 304-305. For Sweden, millions are rounded. 100 Swedish kronen corresponded to 104.115 Swiss francs. The bid price for currency purchases varied between 106.48 in 1939 and a temporary low of 102.59 in 1941.

Überwachung des Warenverkehrs [Swiss Trust Office for Monitoring the Traffic in Goods].[26]

In order to better preserve domestic autonomy, the Swiss Federal Government chose a different path in World War II. The Central Office for Monitoring Imports and Exports [Zentralstelle für die Überwachung der Ein- und Ausfuhr], set up on October 24, 1939, made it possible, with few exceptions, to keep foreign trade free from outside control. However, this was possible only with the cooperation of state agencies and private war economy syndicates in observing the agreements made with the blockade powers. They had to make sure that authorized imports were brought into Switzerland in accordance with guarantee certificates and that these were used in compliance with the obligations Switzerland had accepted. Re-export of goods in unchanged condition was prohibited, even in interrupted transit. Other regulations such as restricted quotas included requirements which exceeded the simple guarantee of a permitted usage of imported goods. This led to a problem with state monitoring, as it amounted in reality to cooperation with the blockades. The export industry depended on the processing of imports and demanded compromises as they were first set down in the War Trade Agreement of April 25, 1940. These solutions were questionable as part of the policy of neutrality, rested on slippery ground, and called forth accusations and pressures by members of the two belligerent parties.

The dilemma of foreign trade policy was based on the fact that goals that were identical in peacetime, namely the preservation of economic viability and thus of the independence of Switzerland, diverged under the force of the blockade and could no longer be reached simultaneously. Economic negotiations had to take care that this collision of interests did not develop into an unbridgeable gulf. The strategy adopted specified that the Swiss Federal Council would act unambiguously, at

---

[26] Concerning the problem of economy and neutrality in World War I see: Heinz Ochsenbein, *Die verlorene Wirtschaftsfreiheit 1914-1918. Methoden ausländischer Wirtschaftskontrollen über die Schweiz.* Bern 1971; Pierre Luciri, *Le prix de la neutralité. La diplomatie secrète de la Suisse en 1914-1915 avec des documents d'archives inédites.* Geneva 1976. Enlightening material is contained in the collection of primary sources: *Diplomatische Dokumente der Schweiz 1848-1945,* Vol. 6: *1914-1918.* (Bern 1981) xl-lii; see also note 36.

least with regard to basic issues. This included the autonomous monitoring of foreign trade on Swiss territory, the willingness to keep trade relations open to all sides, and to reject suggestions opposed to these principles. This was to demonstrate that the blockade was enforced beyond Switzerland's borders and thus Switzerland could not be held responsible for the measures imposed. It was necessary, however, for Switzerland to make concessions in the negotiations regarding the actual implementation of terms in the trade agreements which, as far as measures agreed upon involved sovereignty, also affected the credibility of Swiss neutrality.

Such immediate issues concerning the *politics* of neutrality must be clearly distinguished from anchoring the *economics* of neutrality in international law. Foreign trade corresponds to specific markets and to economic structures of the partner countries; their differences make it impossible to apply in practice the principle of unlimited parity. For good reason, applicable international law does not recognize general economic neutrality, according to which foreign trade policy would have to be handled equally for all belligerent parties and in the same manner as requirements in the military-political arena. Apart from the question concerning war-related materials, the second Hague peace conference of the neutral countries deliberately did not put any restrictions on their domestic trade. The fifth Hague agreement of October 18, 1907 even went so far as to state explicitly in the important article 7 that a neutral power was not obliged "to prevent the export or transit, destined for one or the other of the belligerent parties, of weapons, ammunition and any other item which would be useful for an army or a navy." Article 9 contains the regulation which is in force to this day that restrictions and prohibitions regarding war materials are to be applied equally to all belligerent parties.[27] This equal treatment referred to formal procedures.

---

[27] AS [Official Collection of Federal Laws] (1910), 243-852, especially 527. "Botschaft des Bundesrates and die Bundesversammlung betreffend die Ergebnisse der 1907 im Haag abgehaltenen Zweiten Internationalen Friedenskonferenz vom 28. Dezember 1908," in *Bundesblätter* (1909, I, 1-433, especially 40ff. The Hague Neutrality Agreement for Naval Warfare of October 18, 1907 states in article 6 that the neutral country may not support the belligerents with war materials, while postulating this principle only indirectly for land warfare by allowing private commerce (art. 7); see Hans Rudolf Kurz, "Die Durch- und Ausfuhr von

The scope of shipments did not implicate the neutrality to be observed in exporting war-related materials to the belligerent parties. It was left to the interested countries if and to what extent they wanted to place orders under conditions equally applied. Whether this solution would stand the test was made questionable by the very fragmentary codification of neutrality rights. Switzerland, which could not retreat from foreign trade in an emergency, had to reject economic neutrality that increased its dependence by means of additional restrictions without adequate guarantees.

World War I soon revealed that the Hague conventions did not protect neutral countries against deliberate measures taken by belligerents in order to bring trade with enemy countries under their control. Switzerland was surprised that modern economic warfare was conducted so systematically and comprehensively. However, this all too stereotypical statement remains incomplete. A later interpretation, which considers only the two cited articles of the fifth Hague agreement concerning economic neutrality, wants to forget that the Swiss Federal Council had earlier taken a more consistent stance with regard to the question of war materials. During the Crimean War, which was fought far away, a simple warning was deemed sufficient that Swiss authorities would deny any assistance in the trade in war materials.[28] On May 20, 1859 the Swiss Federal Council decreed an explicit prohibition against the export of weapons, powder, and ammunition through the Swiss-Italian border in the war of Sardinia and France with Austria. As the Federal Government declared on that occasion: "These measures are in full agreement with declared neutrality and thus do not need special justification. The prohibition against weapons and ammunition has its foundation in international law...."[29] This opinion became the precedent for observing Swiss neutrality in the future. When the war between Prussia and Austria, with Italy joining in the south, again called for measures to observe neutrality, the Federal Council once again

Kriegsmaterial aus der Schweiz," in: *Schweizer Allgemeine Militär-Zeitung*, No. 12 (1968), 713-720.

[28] "Kreisschreiben des Bundesrates an die Kantonsregierungen," April 15, 1854, *Bundesblatt* [Federal Journal] (1854), 341-342; cited from here on as Bbl.

[29] "Bericht des Bundesrates an die Bundesversammlung über die im Interesse der Neutralität getroffenen Massregeln," Bbl II (July 1, 1859), 159ff.

prohibited the "export of weapons and war materials in general to the adjoining belligerent countries."[30] Up to that time such a prohibition did not involve measurable sacrifice. Yet in the course of the modernization of weaponry and the introduction of breech-loading guns, Swiss gun production also began to make progress. A statement of the Department of Trade and Customs in 1867 declared that it was for the future to decide "if for us weapons would become an export instead of an import item, as only then would it become possible for this industry to survive."[31] During the German-French war of 1870/71 a conflict of interest had already surfaced between the demands of a clear policy of neutrality and the deviations favored and desired by the new industry. The Swiss Federal Council disregarded the latter and stood fast in its prohibition of exports of weapons and war materials to adjoining belligerent nations. Numerous confiscations of weapons and ammunition showed that the government was serious, and it also applied the prohibition to weapon shipments in transit. In its December 8, 1870 report on the maintenance of Swiss neutrality, the Federal Council specified that private economic interest had to be subordinated to the principle of political neutrality: "Although the Swiss weapons trade suffered under this strict interpretation of neutrality, the Federal Council was still resolved to maintain it as, on the one hand, it conforms to actions taken in earlier similar cases and, on the other, it also conforms more to the popular will."[32]

The provision of the fifth Hague agreement which prohibited the neutral country, but not its inhabitants, from supplying war materials to parties in conflict – this was also the opinion expressed in the message of the Federal Council – was reductionist, a problem that had not gone unnoticed in 1907. Thus the law of neutrality had reached its outer limits, and overstepping it would clearly violate neutrality. However, this did not mean that Switzerland intended to deviate from its more narrowly defined observation of neutrality.[33]

---

[30] "Verordnung über die Handhabung der Neutralität," Bbl (June 16, 1866), 224ff.

[31] Bbl. (1868), II, 198.

[32] Bbl (1870), III, 6-7, 823ff.

[33] "The governments themselves, however, are not allowed to provide the belligerents with weapons, ammunition, or other material needed for warfare, without violating neutrality;" Bbl. (1909), 46. In light of this provision, it was

As in past conflicts, the Federal Council therefore released an ordinance on August 4, 1914 for the prohibition of "the export of weapons, ammunition, and war material to the adjoining belligerent nations".[34] Because the government was surprised by events, supporting measures such as a timely provisioning of the country and an efficient control organization for the buildup of the war economy were missing. France and Great Britain had initiated unimpeded large orders and virtually created a veritable armament industry in Switzerland. The dependence on foreign trade which was already strong led to the fear of serious difficulties if the Swiss Confederation were to maintain its earlier principles of neutrality. The Federal Council retreated to the provisions of the fifth Hague agreement. The autonomously issued export prohibition was only directed against third parties, the new interpretation explained, "while the state itself can grant permission at any time for those exceptions which its own interests demand or are deemed desirable. According to Article 9 of the cited Hague agreement it was only necessary in such cases to guarantee equal application of the principles to the belligerent parties, which we naturally plan to enforce meticulously."[35]

In considering the provisioning of the country, Switzerland had export prohibitions for numerous other categories of goods. Specified exceptions were designed to import goods from abroad which would otherwise have been unavailable. War-related materials, in which the Entente in particular was much interested, became the object of intense controversy, and the requested restrictions and prohibitions were more and more difficult to reconcile with the principle of being even-handed. The search for pragmatic solutions turned into maneuvers detrimental to neutrality and led to accusations of having shielded suspected war profiteers. The export of machine-processed copper goods – a concealed reference to ammunition parts in official specifications of tariff duties

---

therefore improper that in 1939-40 the national powder factory Wimmis supplied powder, destined for ammunition export to the belligerents, to the Werkzeug-maschinenfabrik Oerlikon.

[34] "Verordnung betreffend Handhabung der Neutralität der Schweiz," August 4, 1914, in: AS, (1914), 353ff; 384-385, 483-484.

[35] "Bericht des Bundesrates an die Bundesversammlung über die von ihm auf Grund des Bundesbeschlusses vom 3. August 1914 getroffenen Massnahmen vom 1. Dezember 1914," Bbl. (1914), IV, 707ss., 722-723.

– amounted in 1914 to 241,000 Swiss francs and by 1917 had rapidly increased to more than 166 million. If one includes Italy, more than nine-tenths went to the countries of the Entente.[36] The official request of the Allied governments in May of 1919 that, if requested to do so by the Entente, Switzerland oblige itself in advance to totally sever its economic relations with Germany was rejected as unacceptable by the Swiss Federal Council, which referred to the declaration of neutrality of August 4, 1914.[37]

The provision set down in the Hague agreement continued in force even when Switzerland adopted the stance of differential neutrality after joining the League of Nations. On May 31, 1934 the Federal Council released a prohibition of exports of war materials to Bolivia and Paraguay due to the long-lasting Chaco war. When the League of Nations imposed sanctions on Italy, the Swiss Government also adopted these measures, not only against its neighbor to the south but also against Ethiopia, which put the victim on the same level as the aggressor.[38] The civil war in Spain led to a similar export prohibition which included the Spanish possessions and the Spanish zone of Morocco.[39]

---

[36] *Rückschau über Handel und Industrie der Schweiz 1914-1918*, hrsg. vom Schweizerischen Bankverein (Basel 1919), p. 88; Max Cornaz, *Zum Problem der Wirtschaftsneutralität. Die Handelsverträge der Schweiz im Ersten Weltkrieg.* Dissertation Zürich (Zürich 1952), 78-79. In 1916 no less than 92.7% of copper goods were exported to European members of the Entente. Hans Rudolf Ehrbar, *Schweizerische Militärpolitik im Ersten Weltkrieg. Militärische Beziehungen zu Frankreich vor dem Hintergrund der schweizerischen Aussen- und Wirtschaftspolitik 1914-1918* (Bern 1976), 160, 356, note 463. Ochsenbein, *Die verlorene Wirtschaftsfreiheit*, 326ff.

[37] "Antwortnote des Bundesrates," May 30, 1919, Bbl. (1919), III, 463. Because the *Diplomatische Dokumente der Schweiz 1848-1954*, Vol. 7, part 1 (Bern 1979), 818ff, do not make a reference to this document, the impression is created that the inquiry of France, England, Italy, and the USA of May 19, 1919 had not been responded to according to the provisional decision of the Federal Council of May 20.

[38] Bbl. (1935), I, 167ff; (1935), II, 937ff; (1936), III, 470. AS (1935), 693ff. Regarding the League of Nations and the question of economic neutrality see "Botschaft des Bundesrates an die Bundesversammlung betreffend die Frage des Beitritts zum Völkerbund," August 4, 1919, SA (Bern 1919), 39ff, 71ff.

[39] "Bundesratsbeschluss," August 14, 1936, AS (1936), 637, For revocation see AS (1939), 552.

Because of surging worldwide rearmament during the 1930s, various efforts to curb the international weapons trade within the framework of the League of Nations eventually failed. Although the Swiss popular initiative launched against the private armament industry was defeated in a referendum on February 20, 1938, it led to the acceptance of the parliamentary counterproposal anchored in the new article of the Federal Constitution which established the necessary authority for monitoring of the private sector arms manufacturers. A federal permit was necessary for the production as well as the sale and export of war materials.[40]

That same year, 1938, brought the return to integral neutrality. Switzerland dissolved its obligations of participating in economic sanctions imposed by the League of Nations and was superbly supported in this effort by the Swedish Foreign Minister Richard Sandler whose country, too, insisted that the optional character of observing sanctions was proper.[41] Sensing the threat of a new world war, Switzerland declared its resolve to safeguard its independence based on a consistent policy of neutrality. On April 14, 1939 the Swiss Federal Council approved the draft of a law concerning the maintenance of neutrality; its article 3 prohibited among other things "the export of weapons, ammunition, blasting materials, other war materials, and their components to belligerent nations, as well as any stockpiling of such items in the border areas or for transport across the border."[42] Together with other precautionary measures, the highest authority of the land had thus taken all precautions in order to avoid the unsatisfactory conditions of World War I.

---

[40] Urs Schwarz, "Waffenausfuhrpolitik," in: *Handbuch der schweizerischen Aussenpolitik,* edited by A. Riklin, H. Haug, and H. C. Binswanger (Bern 1975), 813-824; Peter Hurni, "Die Haltung der Schweiz zur Kontrolle des internationalen Waffenhandels im Rahmen des Völkerbundes 1919-1925," in: *Studien und Quellen,* hrsg. vom Schweizerischen Bundesarchiv. Vol. 6 (Bern 1980), 112-130.

[41] Bbl. (1938), I, p. 840ff.; Wolf Ukena, *Die Rückkehr der Schweiz zur integralen Neutralität.* Berlin 1941. This dissertation had been completed before the start of the war and was remarkably factual; the author refers at least in the foreword of November 1940 to the "great political upheavals."

[42] "Verordnung über die Handhabung der Neutralität," April 14, 1939, AS (1939), 810ff.

Inconsistencies in Matters of War
Materials and their Consequences

As soon as it was put to the test, the Federal Council departed from its prohibition against the export of war materials. The reasons for this amazingly rapid return to the unquestionably conflict-laden stance of the fifth Hague Treaty have so far remained obscure. The Federal Council only referred to Allied pressure, yet it had not been maneuvered quite so innocently into its predicament. During the meeting of June 28, 1939, the Political Department stated that Swiss industries more and more frequently approached the Swiss embassy in Paris and requested assistance in obtaining orders from the French authorities for shipments of war material. According to a list of the Military Department that covered the months of September 1938 to May 1939, the following nations were among the largest purchasers of Swiss armament materials: the Netherlands with products worth more than 16 million Swiss francs, France with 13.2 million, Japan with 9.5 million, and Great Britain with 9 million. In contrast, the purchases of Germany amounted merely to 60,000 Swiss francs and those of Italy to only 2,780 Swiss francs. The Political Department requested that the government not plan for any special precautionary measures. Although admitting that it could be expected that in a future war its enemies could consider supplying one country with war materials as a hostile act, the Political Department stressed the economic advantages of armament exports. Its argument tended to ignore reality by claiming that during World War I both parties had purchased war materials from Switzerland at about the same rate and that the available figures showed that these shipments "were made to almost all relevant countries."[43]

Already during the first days of World War Two, France and Great Britain insisted on the fulfillment of the existing supply contracts. In addition, France intended to initiate major orders for ignition parts from

---

[43] "Protokoll der Bundesratssitzung," 30. Juni 1939, Schweizerisches Bundesarchiv, E 1004 1/386. I am particularly grateful to Prof. Dr. Jean-François Bergier and Dr. André Jaeggi for the use of materials they had assembled in preparation of Vol. 13 that covers the years 1939-1941 of the publication series *Diplomatische Dokumente der Schweiz 1848-1945*, to which I resorted for this article.

the watch factories in the Jura. These countries were particularly interested in ignitions because the troops were just being equipped with light anti-aircraft weapons. As it turned out, England and France already had engaged the Swiss production potential for their armaments so deeply that even urgent orders in the interest of Switzerland's own defense were blocked. Although a precarious situation began to emerge already at the war's start not in regard to neutrality rights, but to neutrality politics, the Political Department requested on September 6 that the whole Federal Council should make a secret decision to disregard the published prohibition of exporting war material and to keep the purchasing ability open for both belligerent parties according to still to be determined conditions. To justify the request, the situation of World War One was again embellished:

> These shipments made up an essential part of our exports during that period. To a large extent they served as compensation for imports necessary for the provisioning of our country. They provided work for our mechanical industry during the whole war and prevented the scourge of unemployment from being added to the other difficulties which our people had to endure during those dangerous times. The solution of keeping a perfect equilibrium between the belligerent parties which the Federal Council was able to find in solving the problem of a neutral country supplying war material to belligerent countries thus had actually happy consequences, despite certain criticisms based on ideological considerations.[44]

The demand for work at all costs, which Foreign Minister Pilet-Golaz raised in his controversial speech of June 25, 1940, had already influenced the decision of the Federal Council on September 8, 1939

---

[44] "Protokoll der Bundesratssitzung," 30. Juni, 1939, E 1004 1/386. The request of the Eidgenössische Politische Departement (Political Department), September 6, 1939 has been published in Edgar Bonjour, *Geschichte der schweizerischen Neutralität. Dokumente 1939-1945*, Vol. 8 (Basel 1975), 225-226; the 9-volume work is cited from here on as *Neutralität*. In my opinion, the official reading of Bonjour is insufficiently subjected to critical review when he claims that the weapon exports of World War I had conformed to the neutrality principle of equal treatment of both belligerents. See Edgar Bonjour, "Waffenausfuhr," in: *Die Schweiz und Europa*, Vol. 3 (Basel 1973), 127. Bonjour, *Neutralität*, Vol. 2, 660.

when it dropped the export prohibition. Economic and financial considerations as well as the fear of unemployment and social unrest played a role, but the decision was primarily a solution of an acute conflict of interest. An export prohibition, if it were rigorously applied, would lead to great tensions with the Allies, which were already preparing to put economic pressures on Switzerland. Under these conditions the importance of war materials as a negotiating tool became obvious. As the Political Department admitted, a consistent prohibition would have strengthened the moral position of the country, but the sacrifice was considered to be too great. It was only to be decided whether the standing of Switzerland as a nation of high ethical principles or the pragmatic reason of state would prevail. However, the question of whether a strictly applied policy of neutrality would perhaps also provide a better protection against arbitrary attacks by foreign powers was not considered.

Thus the future direction was set and only the question of how issues would be handled in practice remained to be answered. On September 22, 1939 the Swiss Federal Council established the following conditions for the supply of war materials: the needs of the Swiss army were to have unquestioned precedence, with the exception of certain businesses that were in the interest of the military defense of the country. Raw materials and production equipment needed for its orders were to be made available by the foreign country. The companies were subject to permits and monitoring. Export permits would only be granted for shipments to foreign governments and against cash payments in Switzerland or in exchange for vital goods.[45]

Thus began the actual bargaining between the agents of Allied interests and the authorities in Bern for engaging the Swiss armament industry, especially for the 20-millimeter anti-aircraft cannons produced by the tool factory in Oerlikon that were billed according to the number of pieces produced monthly. On September 22, 1939 the French Ambassador Alphand had received confidential written assurance from Federal Councilor Hermann Obrecht, the head of the Department of Economic Affairs, that the order placed by France before September 2

---

[45] "Protokoll der Bundesratssitzung," 22. September 1939, Bundesarchiv, E 1004 1/389. See note 51.

would, as far as it could be arranged, not be interfered with by Swiss requests. Yet by year's end Switzerland claimed for its own use 120 of the 250 cannons produced in Oerlikon.[46]

Because of mobilization, it was impossible to reach production goals, which led to continuous friction with the French Military Attaché Siméon, who insisted on satisfying the French claim first. There were also threats from Sir David Kelly, the British Minister in Bern, who bluntly stated that his country expected "that the deliveries would at least be made according to the minimum program of orders and, if that were not the case, Great Britain would consider it an unfriendly act."[47] The British Admiralty placed a large set of orders with Oerlikon for the 20-millimeter automatic cannons (type SS). A first order of 520 cannon was delivered in April and a second of 1,000 cannon on September 16, 1939. Added to this were 2,260,000 rounds of ammunition.[48] Numerous subcontractors participated in this order. To satisfy other Allied purchase requests, the available production capacity was used in such a way that it was barely compatible with the directives of September 22, 1939.

The antiquated and inadequate equipment of the Swiss army was particularly noticeable in the area of anti-aircraft defense. In August 1939 attempts were made to requisition for Switzerland's own use cannons made in Oerlikon that had been readied for export to France. However, the Federal Council released the weapons in consideration of the relationship with Switzerland's western neighbor, and even Henri Guisan, the newly appointed commander-in-chief, was unable to persuade the government with his counter arguments.[49] In the interest of the defense of the country, the army had increased its purchase requests,

---

[46] "Letter from Obrecht to Alphand," 22. September, 1939. Bundesarchiv, E 5155 1968/12,2.

[47] "Aktennotiz," 25. November, 1939, signed Fierz, Bundesarchiv, E 5155 1968/12,2. Letter of Fierz to the Eidgenössische Militär Departement [EMD, Military Department], January 16, 1940, ibid., E 5155 1968/12,2.

[48] "Bericht der kriegstechnischen Abteilung an das Eidgenössische Militär Departement," January 16, 1940; letter from Kelly to EMD, January 18, 1940. Bundesarchiv, E 5155 1968/12,2.

[49] "Schreiben Fierz and Oberstleutnant de Blony," 31. Januar, 1940, Bundesarchiv, 5155 1968/12,2.

but the delivery program agreed upon was not implemented. The 280 20-millimeter anti-aircraft cannons, which should have been available in April 1940, were not delivered until the end of October.[50] Considerations of the blockade had priority.

On February 13, 1940, the decision of the Federal Council regarding the production, acquisition and sale, import, and export of war materials was published. This ended the legally problematic situation that in case of violations proper attention could not be given to the domestic guidelines for producers of war materials.[51] Thus allowing the shipments of war materials under certain conditions became public, and now the German side also paid attention. The German envoy and economics specialist Hemmen considered the decision as "very serious" in regard to the policy of neutrality and he observed that as to the delivery of war materials Switzerland had already shown undue preference for the Western powers.[52] The commercial section of the German embassy in Bern knew surprisingly little about the background of the suspension of the strict export prohibition. Thus Hemmen, its chief, wrote to Berlin on March 6, 1940: "It is now presumably true that Switzerland is supplying the enemy countries; yet despite many rumors, at present we do not have exact numbers of the Swiss companies' actual shipments of war materials to enemy countries. But it is equally true that we would receive the same shipments if we were to request them from the Swiss government."[53]

Despite Hemmen's endeavors, at that time the German embassy lacked the necessary personnel for efficient monitoring and also for the processing the results of economic espionage. Hemmen stated that it would be possible to persuade the neutral countries that "the delivery of

---

[50] *Bericht des Chefs des Generalstabes der Armee an den Oberbefehlshaber der Armee über den Aktivdienst 1939-1945* (Bern 1946), 111, 123.

[51] AS (1940), 164ff. To better secure the needs of the Swiss army, the Federal Council passed a resolution on February 16, 1940 concerning the declaration of urgency for orders for war material. "Protokoll der Bundesratssitzung," 16. Februar, 1940, Bundesarchiv, E 1004 1/394.

[52] Schreiben Keller an Hotz, 13. März, 1940, Bundesarchiv, E7110 1967/146, "Frankreich," 821.

[53] "Schreiben Hemmen an Sabath," 6. März, 1940. "Handel mit Kriegsgerät, Schweiz", Vol. 1 HaPol, AA, PA-B.

war materials was incompatible with neutrality". Berlin was alarmed by reports of Switzerland's partiality in economic matters. Yet Hemmen spoke of rumors and intimated to his negotiating partners in Bern that Germany had only to make purchase requests and that it was interested in parity of deliveries. In reality, Switzerland would have had great difficulties in fulfilling additional orders. If Hemmen later appeared to be a particularly unpleasant head of the German team negotiating with Switzerland, it may be because this protégé of Göring could not quite forget that during the first phase of the war he had thoroughly lost out to the agents of the Allies. In March 1940 France's orders for war materials had reached a total of 142.7 million Swiss francs, those of Great Britain 121.2 million, while German orders amounted only to 149,504 Swiss francs.[54] Although more narrowly defined war materials were scarcely purchased, the German Wehrmacht was particularly interested in the acquisition of special machine tools which could be used, among other things, for the production of watch movements with ignition devices and their components. In this case it concerned the production of ignitions for anti-aircraft guns.[55] Since it had been defined in 1907, the term "war material" had greatly expanded so that the transition to the category "goods important for warfare" became accepted. But there was also a marked imbalance concerning tool-making machines; in February 1940 France had actual contracts worth 9.3 million Swiss francs, Great Britain 5 million, and Germany 2.8 million.[56]

Given their advantage, the Allied countries dispensed with restrictions on exports of war materials within the framework of the blockade agreement of April 25, 1940. At that time the German side did not

---

[54] Robert U. Vogler, "Die Wirtschaftsverhandlungen zwischen der Schweiz und Deutschland im Sommer 1940," Lizentiatsarbeit Universität Zürich, 1978, 49; 1983 published as a doctoral dissertation in an expanded form. Josef Bieri, "Die wirtschaftlichen Beziehungen Deutschlands zur Schweiz während der Blitzkriege 1939-1941," Magisterarbeit Universität Konstanz 1971, 82ff., 91ff.

[55] Schreiben des Wirtschaftsrüstungsamt an Auswärtiges Amt, 16. Januar, 1940, "Handel mit Kriegsgerät, Schweiz," Vol. I, HaPol, AA, PA-B.

[56] Vogler, *Wirtschaftsverhandlungen*, 49-50. The figures for purchases of pure aluminum were: Great Britain 7 million Swiss francs, France 1.8 million, Germany 0.5 million.

dispute the right of neutral countries to such exports but insisted however on parity in principle as to the scope of shipments, though this was contradictory insofar as Germany had not placed any corresponding orders. At least legally, Switzerland did not have to feel guilty about violating neutrality. However, the disparity of shipments had assumed such proportions that after the German victory over France it provided an incredibly unfortunate basis for negotiation. The question arises therefore whether the departure from the original prohibition of war material exports had been unwise as far as the policy of neutrality was concerned. One realistic argument states that Switzerland had thereby been spared the humiliation of having to suspend the prohibition under German pressure. The statement that the respective exports had also earlier been primarily to the Allies can counter the reproach of one-sided deliveries to the Allies. To know the pressures of the times is, however, not a justification in itself. The Federal Council was simply too ready to deviate from its principles at the beginning of the war; giving them up resulted in important concessions in the blockade and made Switzerland more vulnerable to blackmail in economic warfare.

Once the situation began to change with the German advance in France, Ambassador Ritter stated to Jean Hotz, the Swiss head of the delegation, and to Minister Fröhlicher at the beginning of negotiations in Berlin that in Germany's view Switzerland seemed to be "one large armament factory working almost exclusively for England and France". It would not be permitted "that Switzerland use one more kilogram of German coal for the production and delivery of industrial products destined for England or France".[57] In the second half of June Germany blocked its coal deliveries to Switzerland. On June 18 Hemmen telegraphed to Berlin the concessions reported to him by Director Hotz in Bern. The total reorientation of war material exports was indicated in the following statement:

> Federal Council ready to supply us with unlimited war material to the extent of Switzerland's ability. Specified list of the shipments accepted here from the order list we handed to Fierz follows by courier and amounts to 35 million francs plus 8 million Oerlikon orders. For

---

[57] Aktenvermerk, 30. Mai, 1940, signed Ritter. "Schweiz, Handakten Clodius," HaPol, AA, PA-B.

this they expect us to supply steel, zinc, and chemical materials for tracer ammunition, but are prepared to supply here the necessary copper, brass, aluminum, tin, and nickel. Until the end of our negotiations all deliveries of war material orders to enemy powers have temporarily been halted. Weapons delivery for Holland, Belgium, and Norway are also subject to this blockade. It has been made sure that they are in no way shipped to London. We are able to take over finished weapons as well as the production capacity reserved for these countries.[58]

The Swiss offer made in this agreement was a tactical attempt to adapt the given untenable trade policy to the changes in Europe and to create a new base for negotiation. Without such an adaptation it was impossible to expect demands in favor of Switzerland to be accepted by Germany. Minister Fröhlicher, the Swiss Ambassador to Berlin, had been alarmed by the threat that the Swiss delegation should be made aware that, in case no agreement could be reached, "Germany did not care at all about trade with Switzerland. Beyond that, it could still have quite other consequences for Switzerland."[59] It became possible to find a solution under the pressures of the counter-blockade. Hemmen dramatized the forced concessions in his telegram. These conformed for the most part to the new situation. From now on, shipments of war material flowed to Axis-controlled regions – an abrupt turn which seriously undermined the credibility of the Swiss policy of neutrality. German orders for war-related materials soon exceeded the volume of those placed earlier by the Allies. Emil Bührle and his subcontractors welcomed that the German navy and air force each requested one thousand 20-millimeter Oerlikon cannons, because they were afraid of being stuck with still unpaid orders from the Western powers. Thus the export balance sheet for armaments and quota-subject goods became one-sided. The total value of goods in these categories exported to Germany amounted in 1942 to 353 million Swiss francs, while the Allied countries had to be satisfied with exports in the amount of 13.8 million francs; the ratio for 1943 was 425 million to 17.8 million Swiss francs.[60]

---

[58] Telegramm Hemmen an Auswärtiges Amt, 18. Juni, 1940, ibid.

[59] Aufzeichnung, 3. Juni, 1940, signed Ritter, ibid.

[60] Aktenvermerk, 25. Oktober, 1940, signed Schüller. "Handel mit Kriegsgerät, Schweiz," Vol. 2, HaPol, AA, PA-B. Klaus Urner, "Die schweizerisch-deutschen Wirtschaftsbeziehungen während des Zweiten Weltkrieges," in: *Neue Zürcher*

Would the two belligerent sides have put less pressure on Switzerland if it had consistently maintained its export prohibition on armaments? In this speculative form the question can hardly be answered. In retrospect, the deficiencies in handling the politics of foreign trade are quite visible and today argue for a strict adherence to the principles of the law concerning war materials which became effective on February 1, 1973. Based on considerations of expediency and in the interest of the armament industry, the Federal Government had given free rein to the developments of the summer of 1939, although it was not unaware of its possible effect in case of war. When the prohibition on exporting war materials was already abandoned on September 8, 1939, the requirements of a more narrowly defined economic neutrality had been viewed as only an ethical principle. Upholding on the grounds of material sacrifice was not even seriously considered. The Federal Council, therefore, was unable to insist on the precedence of orders made in the interest of the country's own defense. This lack of circumspection contrasted with the farsighted preparatory measures taken by Federal Councilor Obrecht, who built up an efficient organization of the war economy.[61] He was convinced that a strong private armament industry would also strengthen Swiss defense capability, yet this former President of the Board of the Weapons Factory Solothurn lacked the clear-sightedness which otherwise marked his outlook.

The Blockade Agreements and Their
Implications for Neutrality Policy

In economic warfare the various parties cared only for their own vital interests, and Switzerland could not rely on a secret solidarity of democratically minded forces. Because the Swiss (with some few exceptions already noted) sympathized with the Western powers, the

---

Zeitung, No. 734 (November 27); No. 745 (December 2), No. 756 (December 6, 1968).

[61] Hermann Böschenstein, *Bundesrat Obrecht 1882-1940* (Solothurn 1982), 241ff. Federal Councillor Obrecht retired on June 20, 1940, but because of heart problems experienced late in 1939 he had been unable to fulfill his duties as Head of the Federal Department of Economic Affairs.

hostility of these powers led in 1939 and again towards the end of the war to repeated disillusionment. It was scarcely possible to rely on the judgment of foreigners as to whether Switzerland was violating its neutrality. Both belligerent sides measured the value of neutrality according to their perceived advantages and disadvantages. Accordingly, they responded with appreciative pronouncements, verbal attacks, and massive pressure. Both the course of the war, and also the tone used by both sides towards the neutral countries, was volatile.

During the first phase that lasted from the war's start to the attack on France, Germany behaved properly, even courteously, towards Switzerland. Hemmen, the head of the German negotiating team, declared to Federal Councilor Obrecht on September 6, 1939 that his country wanted to arrange the fullest possible maintenance of existing economic relations and to solve problems amicably.[62] Soon afterwards the Reich's Government stated via the "Deutsche Nachrichten Büro" [German Information Office] that it had no objection to neutral countries continuing the "normal exchange of goods" with enemy states. Neutral nations would take a non-neutral stance, however, if they "would permit other countries to force them into actual restrictions or formal controls directed against the continuation of normal exchange and transit of goods from neutral states to Germany."[63] This addition unmasked the alleged friendly reticence as a tactical maneuver and warned the neutral countries, which at first were less able to exert effective pressure on Germany than on the Allies. With its prompt shipments, Germany settled the clearing arrears of 80 million Swiss francs from before the war according to the agreement of October 24, 1939, and in the spring of 1940 Germany received a credit balance of 40 million Swiss francs, subject to Swiss restrictions.

The Allied blockade powers had superior control of the ocean and conducted their economic warfare with ruthless force. They claimed that shortening the war's duration presented neutral countries with the best opportunity for rapid recovery. At first, shipments of goods were only

---

[62] Telegramm Hemmen an Auswärtiges Amt, 7. September, 1939. "Handelsvertragsverhältnis zu Deutschland," Vol. 8, HaPol 11a, Schweiz,19/2 AA, PA-B.

[63] *Neue Zürcher Zeitung*, II, No. 1636 (September. 13, 1939). The "Deutsche Nachrichtenbüro" [German Intelligence Office] cited as source the semi-official *Deutsche diplomatisch-politische Korrespondenz.*

released after the recipient signed a declaration that the imported goods would be used in Switzerland and would not be re-exported in any shape or form. These so-called "undertakings" disregarded the autonomous domestic monitoring and in the long run would have meant widespread paralysis of Swiss foreign trade. Only after more than five months of negotiations, conducted with interruptions in Paris and London, did Switzerland accept a blockade agreement, in the War Trade Agreement of April 25, 1940. It had resisted pressure more energetically than Belgium, the Netherlands, or Sweden, which had already signed similar agreements on December 7, 1939. Apart from the principle that imports were not to be re-exported in an unchanged condition, Switzerland agreed to the restriction that certain goods on List A could not be exported at all. These were mainly goods that Switzerland had to import for its own use. But it also comprised products which were independent of the blockade, including goods such as peas and beans, pigs, and walnut wood. The list of prohibited goods was materially of little importance and mainly a matter of principle.

Yet Lists B1 and B2 in particular indicated that the Federal Council had gone beyond passive tolerance and had agreed to active participation in the blockade. The goods categorized on the first list could be exported as in the past to countries outside Europe, the Western powers, to Belgium, Luxembourg, Greece, Ireland, Iceland, Portugal, and Turkey, while exports to "other countries" were to be restricted to the normal flow based on the trade statistics of 1938. The second list contained additional restrictions for exports to Germany, among them on products such as milk, cheese, fruit and domestic cattle of purely Swiss origin.[64] Certain restrictions were directed against countries not listed individually and enabled the Western powers to camouflage the division into "good" and "bad" neutral countries. After the attack on Denmark and Norway, the list of "bad neutrals" was expanded, so that shortly before the acceptance of the blockade agreement a new requirement had to be fulfilled. Federal Councilor Obrecht stated in a confidential report: "We finally agreed that, in view of the recent events, Norway and Sweden have to be deleted from the list of good neutral

---

[64] W.N. Medlicott, *The Economic Blockade*, Vol. I (London 1978), 223-237. This book, a reprint of the original edition published in two volumes in 1952/1959, is still the most comprehensive description of Allied blockade policy.

countries."[65] War materials did not appear on any of the lists. Just like other goods important to the war or mere "peacetime goods", they remained totally free to be exported to all countries. Certificates of origin guaranteed an effective export control.

With the replacement of the "undertakings" by official "Guarantee Certificates", the monitoring of imports and exports was again done fully within the country and by Swiss authorities. The guarantee certificates were the basis for the issuance of the navicerts – that is escort passes – which permitted the passage of overseas goods through the blockade. Switzerland hoped to secure its imports until a repeal of the agreement, which was possible at any time, and it had also been enabled to export to Germany goods which could not be produced without a further processing of goods that depended on the blockade. The Swiss delegation had also been assured orally that no Swiss companies would be put on the blacklist for their trade with Germany so long as they adhered to the stipulated regulations. This agreement lasted until 1942.[66] Although the treaty itself became rapidly outdated by the events of the war, it remained legally in force and retained its historical importance as a counterpart to the clearing agreement of August 9, 1940 between Germany and Switzerland.

As Germany had drawn the limits for allegedly non-neutral behavior very narrowly at the beginning of the war, this development was viewed with mistrust in Berlin. Shortly after the blockade agreement had been reached, Viktor Bruns, the director of the Institute for Foreign Public Law and International Law [Institut für ausländisches öffentliches Recht und Völkerrecht] sharply attacked Switzerland's stance.[67] Apart from the "positive law of contract" he referred to the "unwritten common law

---

[65] "Bericht und Antrag des Eidgenössischen Volkswirtschaftdepartementes an den Bundesrat," 22. April, 1940, signed Obrecht. Private files of Dr. Heinrich Homberger, III. 9; Archiv für Zeitgeschichte (AfZ), Eidgenössische Technische Hochschule, Zürich.

[66] Robert Kohli, "Die Schwarzen Listen im Zweiten Weltkrieg," taped lecture presented to the Freundes- und Fördererkreis des Archivs für Zeitgeschichte, Zürich, on April 28, 1977.

[67] Victor Bruns, *Der britische Wirtschaftskrieg und das geltende Seekriegsrecht* (Berlin 1940). This publication is based on a lecture of April 29, 1940 and considers in this greatly expanded version the developments until August 1940.

of neutrality" and declared: "The neutral countries do not have the excuse that there is no obligation of neutrality in the economic sector. Their basic duty is a non-partisan and equal attitude towards the belligerents' conduct of war even in the area of economic warfare".[68] A neutral country could only claim the acknowledgment of its neutrality by a belligerent if the country itself as well as the other belligerents respected its neutrality. Bruns not only denounced the enemy for continued disregard of the rights of neutral countries, but also insinuated that Switzerland had let itself become a direct tool of British warfare. For the international lawyer from Berlin this legitimated the use of repressive measures: "If the neutral country tolerates such violations, the other belligerent party has the right to repressive measures against the enemy as well as against the neutral country."[69]

Dietrich Schindler, a professor of international law in Zürich, rejected Bruns' claims, not least based on the observation that "similar reproaches could today also be raised by the British side."[70] Bruns assigned the belligerent parties not only certain obligations, but also claimed that they had certain duties toward neutral countries. Because of actions Germany had taken, his theses had already lost their value as an alibi for the responsible authorities in Berlin even before they were published. As soon as Germany had a chance after the armistice with France, they showed little regard for arguments derived from international law and pressured Switzerland by means of the counter-blockade.

When on July 29, 1940 the chief negotiators for Switzerland, Jean Hotz, Heinrich Homberger, and Robert Kohli declared in Berlin that Switzerland could do nothing that contradicted neutrality, Ministerial Councilor Seyboth responded that the idea of neutrality was now undergoing change and that "it should be left to the science of international law to re-examine the question of neutrality after the war." The new tactics that no neutral country should be surprised "if we defend our

---

[68] Ibid , 68-69.

[69] Ibid., 73.

[70] Brief D. Schindler an C.E. Koechlin und R. Kohli, of 9. Oktober, 1941. I thank Prof. Dietrich Schindler, Zollikon, for granting me the use of his father's files. In judging Schindler's position one must keep in mind that the Political Department in Bern gave him information, but not access to the files of the Department. Dietrich Schindler, "Wirtschaftspolitik und Neutralität" in: *Schweizerische Juristenzeitung*, 14 (1942), 209-214; 15 (1942), 225-231.

interest as ruthlessly as England" were announced with brutal clarity.[71] The euphoria of the "Blitz" victory accelerated the change in attitude, and the demands of the German negotiating delegation were accordingly excessive. For Berlin, economic neutrality had become a closed subject, but it was determined to exploit Swiss production capacity all the more for its own war economy. However, there was disappointment at the British Ministry of Economic Warfare about the lack of delivery of the ordered war materials. With increasing self-confidence London now insisted, quite differently from before, that the requirements of neutrality in the economic sector be scrupulously observed.

Despite this difficult phase of forced radical change, Switzerland did not subject its foreign trade policy to any outside dictation nor did it engage in blind opportunism. The blockade agreement contained the guidelines according to which the concessions agreed upon also were to be enforced toward the Axis, without conceding the principles which Switzerland defended. This was achieved despite the coal blockade and other threats. Switzerland successfully resisted the unreasonable demand that it break trade relations with Great Britain and its colonies. It kept foreign trade open in all directions as far as possible, and assigned the highest value to the blockade agreement with England, particularly because of imports from overseas.

Although the Federal Council had consented to prohibitions of exports to Western powers, in view of the encirclement it was possible to maintain the principle, at least towards the outside world, of Switzerland's non-participation in the Axis export blockade. It was up to Germany in concert with Italy to secure controls of Swiss exports so long as the encirclement made that possible. Germany initiated the escort document system as a counterpart to the navicerts. A first list comprised those goods for which export was prohibited, except if an escort document had been requested from the German or Italian embassy in Bern. Armaments and other war-related goods the Axis powers claimed for themselves. For certain luxury items there were no restrictions at all. The list of free goods was of small importance. Swiss table fruits, embroideries, or household machines interested neither Berlin nor London. The remaining goods, which amounted in value to

---

[71] Aktenvermerk, 30. Juli, 1941, signed Sabath. "Handelsvertragsverhältnisse zu Deutschland," Vol. 9, HaPol 11a Schweiz 19/2, AA, PA-B.

about 70 percent of normal exports, could be traded within the framework of the usual commerce based on the years 1937-38, yet German requests were to be given preference. A mixed commission coordinated these concessions with Great Britain, which at that time still agreed to an increase in the quotas stipulated in the blockade agreement.[72]

It was nevertheless impossible to fulfill the regulations of the fifth Hague Treaty which Switzerland had always accepted as the outer limit. Securing survival had precedence, but it was not sufficient to describe the German concessions achieved by negotiations without also clearly indicating those made in return. A short-term violation was Switzerland's decision of July and August 1940 to stop on its own accord the export of war materials to Great Britain because the Axis had not yet brought the Geneva-Annemasse rail line (and thus the export route via unoccupied France to Spain and Portugal) under its control. The concession was made to gain important time for negotiations after the Germans had demanded a total cessation of commerce with England.[73]

More serious was the fact that the agreement of August 9, 1940 between Germany and Switzerland was based on an additional element: a clearing credit of 150 million Swiss francs. An attempt to operate with credits had already been made in early 1940 in negotiations with England. The plan called for a loan of up to 100 million francs in the form of private bank credits. The credit deal was supposed to help

---

[72] Homberger, *Schweizerische Handelspolitik*, 46ss. Bonjour, *Neutralität*, Vol. 6, 201ss, 213ff.

[73] Schreiben Hotz an Bonna, 15. August, 1940, BAr E 2001 (D) 2, 137. In early September 1940 a sabotage platoon of the German intelligence had blasted the viaduct of Evires so that the only rail connection to Vichy France was interrupted. The note by Lahousen of Oct. 11, 1940, reproduced by Fuhrer, according to which this act of sabotage caused the Federal Council to issue an export prohibition of weapons from Oerlikon via Lisbon to England is erroneous, as this measure had been taken two and a half months earlier, during the second half of June; see Hans Rudolf Fuhrer, *Spionage gegen die Schweiz. Die geheimen deutschen Nachrichtendienste gegen die Schweiz im Zweiten Weltkrieg 1939-1945*, (Frauenfeld 1982), 28-29. The rail connection was re-established soon thereafter and Germany insisted in Vichy that the transit prohibition be observed there too. Aktenvermerk vom 11. November, 1940, signed Ritter. "Akten betr. Schweiz," Vol. 8, HaPol Wiel, AA, PA-B. The Swiss delegation also successfully rejected the German demand to declare a total export prohibition to France.

suffering industrial sectors such as textiles, whereby the real emergency situation remained concealed – that England had developed a great need for war materials and was hardly interested in Swiss peacetime exports. The credits for creating work outside of the industrial branches that were important for warfare would have enabled Great Britain to get its orders for armaments better filled by this foreign currency relief. According to the then-prevailing opinion this unfortunate connection precluded state participation in these credits, and the project did not succeed due to conditions set by the private bank consortium and because of the events of the war.[74]

The analogy with the situation regarding the credit problem a few months later is obvious, although the credit agreement with Great Britain had been avoided. For the German orders of war material envisioned, the ordinary clearing means were insufficient. For this reason Germany wanted to totally eliminate the existing system of value limitations in order to purchase only war materials. The Swiss negotiating team pursued diametrically opposed interests. Because all export industries were dependent on work and earnings, Germany had to be obligated to continuous delivery of provisions such as coal, iron, fertilizers, and fuels; to the inclusion of the "invisibles"; to an acceptable arrangement in the treaty on tourist traffic; and to similar requirements. Neither the readiness for comprehensive deliveries of war materials nor a generously arranged transit traffic through the Gotthard and Simplon tunnels were sufficient to persuade Germany to agree. Only the introduction of credit as effective compensation made possible the conclusion of the momentous treaty of August 9, 1940, which was supposed to be effective until the end of June 1941. Since according to the agreement of June 22, 1940, 28 million Swiss francs had already been paid to the unrestricted account of the Freie Reichsbank in connection with the earlier "coal and iron account", the 150 million Swiss franc credit (which included about 2 million Swiss francs which had accrued in the travel account) actually amounted only to an additional 124 million Swiss francs for new currency certificates. An additional contingency was agreed to – that each month Switzerland

---

[74] *Kriegswirtschaft*, 88; Bonjour, "Bericht Thurnheer an Motta," 18. Januar, 1940, *Neutralität*, Vol. 9, 191.

could obtain an additional eleven million in goods if the purchases should exceed normal values. In this way it became possible to oblige Germany to issue currency certificates also for goods that were related more to peace than war, up to a value limit that was agreed upon for each position and amounted to at least 40 percent of the original peacetime exports. Among the German promises the coal deliveries, which were to reach a volume of 870,000 tons by the end of 1940, deserve special attention.[75]

The whole agreement depended on the granting of credit, but this fateful coupling later had the effect that increased credit volume and a rise in armament exports went hand in hand. It was hoped that the first clearing credit would lead to additional exports to Germany of weapons and ammunition valued at 100 million Swiss francs, of aluminum for up to 20 million, and also would increase exports of machines and agricultural products to about 40 million Swiss francs.[76] But already in October 1940 the navy, air force, and army announced additional orders for war materials amounting to 261 million Swiss francs. In the provisional protocol of February 7, 1941 Switzerland granted a new clearing credit of 165 million Swiss francs and received as compensation primarily the assurance of continued German coal deliveries at the current level of about 150,000 tons per month. The efforts to break the counter-blockade yielded their first results with the increase of certain export quotas and the expansion of the free list.[77]

On January 28, 1941, Göring's air force had already informed the Foreign Ministry of new and urgent acquisition requests, which would require an expenditure of 344 million Swiss francs in 1941. Disavowing the agreement just concluded, Germany now requested an increase in

---

[75] "Deutsch-schweizerisches Verrechnungsabkommen," 9. August, 1940, Vol. 1 HaPol *Verträge* 8 Switzerland, AA, PA-B. For details see the agreement on payments for goods, travel, insurance, banking, the transfer agreement, the regulations of the clearing traffic, together with the exchange of letters regarding the rules of the counter-blockade; these constitute the content of the agreement of August 9, 1940.

[76] "Protokoll der Bundesratssitzung," 13. August, 1940. Bundesarchiv E 1004 1/400; Bonjour, *Neutralität,* Vol. 8, 164.

[77] Protokoll, 7. February, 1941, signed Hotz, Seyboth. Schweiz, Vol. 8, HaPol Wiehl, AA, PA-B

the credit to a minimum of 650 million Swiss francs. In the agreement of July 18, 1941 Switzerland even made the concession of a credit limit of 850 million Swiss francs and extended the agreement to the end of 1942 with the hope that this might secure at least the promised supplies of coal, iron, lubricating oil, and gasoline for an extended time. In December 1941 the German Minister Köcher had to admit in Bern that the mineral oil agreement could no longer be adhered to. By early 1942 even the coal deliveries greatly lagged behind the contractual agreement. In mid-July 1942 Hemmen predicted the reduction of the iron exports from 14,000 to 6,500 tons monthly but nevertheless demanded a credit increase to unlimited amounts. By the end of the contract period at the end of December 1942 the German arrears amounted to 960,000 tons of coal, 130,000 tons of iron and 78,000 tons of fuel and mineral oils. Switzerland risked failure of negotiations, and a period without a contract began on January 15, 1943. Three months later the scandalous discovery surfaced in Bern that the credit limit of 850 million Swiss francs, set in July 1941, had been unlawfully exceeded. The Germans had issued currency certificates up to about 1,350 million Swiss francs and Bern's Commercial Section had discovered this despicable maneuver much too late. The limit had been reached, and the agreement of June 23, 1943 now reflected reduced exports of Swiss war materials as well as increasing easements in the counter-blockade. However, the notorious coal credit, which provided that an advance of fifty francs was to be granted for each ton of coal supplied and to be repaid only after the war, also dates from that time. The reductions took place step by step so that the agreement of June 29, 1944 provided for war material exports that were a mere 20 percent of those of 1942. When the Americans reached Switzerland via Grenoble, the counter-blockade and the concomitant restrictions were declared invalid shortly thereafter on September 7, 1944.[78]

The developments between August 1940 and early 1943 clearly show how the transfer guarantee favored exports of armaments more and more directly. Although the original concept of this credit system had been assigned a different function within the framework of the

---

[78] The information is based on the dossier "Schweiz," Vol. 8, HaPol Wiehl, AA; "Aufzeichnungen über Diplomatenbesuche," Juli-Dezember 1942, Büro des Staatssekretärs, AA; Handel mit Kriegsgerät, Schweiz, Vol. 2 HaPol. AA, PA-B.

overall agreements, Germany forced it more and more into the service of unlimited armament requests. The granting of credit to Italy in this respect was also quite clear. Despite the war economy agreement of June 22, 1940, by the end of July the Italian government requested a clearing advance based on the German example. By an exchange of notes of August 23, the National Bank opened a credit of 75 million Swiss francs and the Federal Government provided additional security for the advance by a bank consortium in the amount of 125 million Swiss francs. It was known that Italy wanted to use the credit primarily for the purchase of war materials which it had ordered from the Oerlikon factory as well as for aluminum and machine tools. When Italy demanded another credit in December 1940 and was granted the desired increase to 150 million Swiss francs in March 1941, it again acquired guns, ammunition, and machine tools indispensable to the war effort.[79] Switzerland again set a number of conditions in its favor and received assurance on transit and for raw material deliveries for goods such as pyrite, hemp, and aluminum oxide. Yet the actual Italian use of the credit cannot be hidden. In this instance the handling of foreign trade policy violated the neutrality laws, which did not permit such a one-sided engagement of a neutral country in favor of only one of the belligerent parties, particularly as to armaments. From the Swiss point of view the credits served its economic survival and thus its right to self-determination. It is in the nature of Janus-faced advances that they cannot be judged only from one perspective.

Breaking the Counter-blockade
and New Dependencies

Attempts to maintain trade with the Allies, whether through official or secret paths, were partly successful despite the Axis encirclement. In July 1940 the High Command of the German Wehrmacht had learned that the Hispano-Suiza company in Geneva had sold the license for its 20-millimeter aircraft cannons to the still-neutral USA and that there were plans for moving armament factories and their specialist workers

---

[79] Schreiben Hotz an Rüegger, 6. September, 1940, Bundesarchiv E 7110 1967/32, Italy 900. Bonjour, *Neutralität*, Vol. 9, 100ff.

abroad. On August 30, the Swiss Federal Council made the traffic in inventions and licenses related to war materials subject to permits, a measure which was not taken as independently as its justification implied.[80]

In early 1941 German intelligence traced another gap. France did the checking of letter and small parcel mail, not the Axis powers themselves. In this manner, watch jewels, watch springs, and ejection clutches for anti-aircraft guns found their way in large quantities primarily through Italy to the USA and from there to England. On June 13, 1941 the Swiss Federal Council prohibited the export of goods of all types by letter mail, which meant that the principle of leaving the implementation of the blockade exclusively to the Axis was no longer fully upheld. Without this measure the Axis would have seriously impeded the remaining letter traffic. According to David Gordon, the head of the blockade section in the US Foreign Economic Administration, it had even been possible to smuggle out of the country precision instruments that were used for boring the jewels, together with some expert workers, so that a processing industry could be established later in the Allied area.[81]

Swiss trade relations with the Allies remained secondary so long as the Allies were unable to replace Germany as the principal supplier. Under these circumstances, the efforts of Swiss negotiators to provide Great Britain through the counter-blockade with important war-related goods in order to get urgently needed raw materials in return as part of a compensation deal remained fruitless. After the USA had entered the war and became aware of the large credit increase in favor of Germany, the Allies insisted more and more that Switzerland reduce armament deliveries to their enemies. This, in truth, reduced Berlin's readiness to grant Swiss requests for loosening the counter-blockade. A modest

---

[80] "Schreiben OKW [Wehrmacht High Command] an Auswärtiges Amt," 27. Juli, 1940, signed Becker. "Handelsvertragsverhältnisse zu Deutschland," Vol. 9, HaPol 11a Schweiz, 19/2, AA, PA-B. Bbl. (1940), II, 1214-1215.; AS (1940), 1612.

[81] Excerpt from the article published in *Harper's Magazine,* "How We Blockaded Germany," (April 26, 1945); Aktenbestand Dr. Heinrich Homberger III, 16, Archiv für Zeitgeschichte. Aufzeichnung vom 6. Januar, 1941, signed Schüller; Schweiz, Vol. 8, HaPol Wiehl, AA, PA-B. AS (1941), 670; Bbl. (1941), 901.

accommodation in this respect did occur, but London's already minimal interest in it was fading. Minister Hans Sulzer's mission in late 1942 encountered the same impasse, which even an offer of credit in the amount of 200 million Swiss francs could not overcome. Germany's actions in exceeding the credit limits, and its simultaneous failure to fulfill its delivery obligations, made it easier for Switzerland to reduce its armament exports as of July 1943, a reduction that eventually extended to all goods important to the war. From the perspective of London and Washington this occurred much too slowly and led to repeated long interruptions in imports and, as at the beginning of the war, to massive pressure by means of blacklists. In the agreement concluded by Paul Keller in London on December 19, 1943 it was at least possible to restart the supply of food from overseas, with the obligation to restrict still further exports to Germany. As they did a year earlier, the Allies promised not to discriminate against Swiss companies, particularly if they fulfilled the agreed-upon quotas. However, in 1944 more and more companies were forced to sign a guarantee despite the Swiss Federal Council's prohibition. Of the approximately 15,000 blacklisted companies and individuals from all non-belligerent countries, some 10 percent had their headquarters in Switzerland, among them numerous subsidiaries of German companies. The demand that owners of a company had to declare a desire for an Allied victory and to make their books available at all times to British authorities or their designated accountants led to untenable conditions and made Swiss governmental authority questionable.[82]

These pressures undeniably quickened the distancing from Germany in the economic sector. On the other hand, agitators such as the British Commercial Attaché Lomax lacked understanding for the difficult position of the small isolated country, as well as for the efforts it made to regain increased economic independence. Distrust was deepened even more by the less than convincing handling of external financial relations. In April 1939 the Swiss National Bank had voiced its support for declaring an export prohibition for gold in case of war. However, the

---

[82] Robert Kohli, "Die Schwarzen Listen im Zweiten Weltkrieg," taped lecture of April 28, 1977, Archiv für Zeitgeschichte. Regarding the course of trade relations with the Allies, see Bonjour, *Neutralität*, Vol. 6, 289ss.; Homberger, *Schweizerische Handelspolitik*, 77ff, 98ff.

Federal Council preferred to keep the gold trade free of regulations and thus made Switzerland particularly attractive as a financial trading country. Here too, Switzerland came into an unfavorable light when it was suspected that it had become a purchaser of looted German gold. The blocking of gold deposits made by the Swiss National Bank in New York, as well as stern warnings, finally led to the Federal Council's decision of December 7, 1942 to make the import and export of gold subject to permission by the National Bank. However, its management lacked sufficient political farsightedness and perseverance to avoid the purchasing obligation from Germany. On March 2, 1945, and thus much too late, followed the restriction of free currency exchange (designed to prevent looted money, which among other items had been amassed in extermination camps, from being put into circulation through the neutral currency).[83]

Negotiations with the Allied delegation led by the American Lauchlin Currie, in which France participated for the first time since 1940, again demonstrated how little the victors of 1945 appreciated economic neutrality. The negotiators now considered Switzerland's adherence to it as truly immoral. They demanded the immediate termination of trade with Germany, the blocking of transit, and the fulfillment of the recommendations of the Bretton Woods Conference. The Federal Council again opted for *realpolitik*, at which Federal Councilor Stampfli bitterly remarked about the harsh Allied conditions that, "We were never as badly treated by the Germans as we are now by the Allies."[84] The rapid collapse of the Third Reich's power, however, allowed solutions which led to the Currie Agreement of March 8, 1945 without a formal renunciation of neutrality. This eliminated in principle the import blockade to the extent that it ceased to apply to quota-limited scarce goods. Yet Switzerland's supply situation remained precarious, and only after the Washington Agreement of 1946 could one speak of a turn towards normalization.[85]

---

[83] AS (1942), 1137, Bbl. (1943), I, 396-397; Bbl. (1945), I, 51-52. Regarding the question of the looted gold and related publications by Marco Durrer, Werner Rings, and Robert Vogler see Klaus Urner, "Emil Puhl und die Schweizerische Nationalbank. Zur Kontroverse um das deutsche Raubgold im Zweiten Weltkrieg," in: *Schweizerische Monatshefte*, 7/8 (July/August 1985): 623-631.

[84] Bonjour, *Neutralität*, Vol. 6, 376.

[85] Daniel Frei, "Das Washingtoner Abkommen von 1946. Ein Beitrag zur Geschichte der schweizerischen Aussenpolitik zwischen dem Zweiten Weltkrieg und dem Kalten Krieg," in: *Schweizerische Zeitschrift für Geschichte* (1969), 567-

Edgar Bonjour's claim that Switzerland never disregarded the obligations incurred by a neutral country as set down in the Hague Convention requires some qualification.[86] Yet the Swiss government successfully rejected disastrous demands which could easily have been the beginning of surrender. Even a critical evaluation must recognize the enormous achievement of a Swiss foreign trade policy that, in spite of an extended double blockade, assured the Swiss people's economic survival. It also strengthened the long-term military defense readiness which, above all, vouches for the credibility of Swiss neutrality.

---

619. Marco Durrer, *Die schweizerisch-amerikanischen Finanzbeziehungen im Zweiten Weltkrieg*. Bern 1984.

[86] Bonjour, *Neutralität*, Vol. 6, 409: "Switzerland disregarded neither the legal obligations for neutral countries as set down in the Hague Convention, nor did it break the Gotthard agreement or other treaties."

PART TWO

DEFENSE

III: THE SWISS ARMY WAS READY:

Reasons Germany Dropped "Operation Switzerland"

Hans Senn

Was everything done that was humanly possible to restrain a potential enemy from carrying out a planned attack on Switzerland? There are various answers to this question.

Build-up of the Army

First the improvement of Switzerland's instrument of defense shall be considered which at the beginning of World War Two was still seriously deficient. To remedy the situation, almost four billion francs (of that time's value) were allocated. More than one billion francs were spent for weapons and ammunition, 345 million for aircraft, 1.2 billion for troop, reserve, and replacement material as well as for clothing and equipment and, finally, 657 million francs were spent on permanent fortifications. To obtain today's value, these numbers have to be multiplied by at least a factor of ten. Over the years considerable progress was made in the areas of close combat, anti-tank defenses, artillery support, and anti-aircraft guns. The number of automatic weapons tripled, anti-tank weapons increased sixfold, the mobility and efficiency of the artillery intensified, and some 3,000 new anti-aircraft guns were purchased. The number of combat aircraft increased from 216 to 530, although only 83 of these were equivalent to the combat aircraft of the German Wehrmacht.[1] The lack of armored vehicles forced the army to adopt a rigid defense posture. The proposal to stock chemical warfare agents to retaliate against possible gas attacks had to be dropped after practical tests and first preparatory measures revealed great difficulties. Too much money, furthermore, would be needed to stock

---

[1] Report by the Chief of the General Staff on the active service, Materials section.

sufficient quantities of these warfare means that might possibly never be used.[2]

At the war mobilization of 1939, some 420,000 soldiers and members of the Women's Auxiliary Service, that is about ten percent of the Swiss population, reported for service. By the end of 1941, the army was in a position to call up some 500,000 soldiers and 300,000 auxiliary forces. If one adds the local defense forces, some 20 percent of the population was engaged in defensive tasks.[3] Thus soldiers were not lacking, although their combat readiness admittedly varied greatly. During the war years the operating expenses of the army, including field fortifications, amounted to more than 4 billion francs in the currency value of that time. To save money, it was necessary to significantly reduce the personnel in active service in times of a diminished threat. The Federal Council and the army leadership hereby took the risk, however, that in an emergency not all servicemen might be able to reach their reporting stations in time.

Since first priority was given to fortifying the terrain, the training of troops was greatly neglected until the deployment of all army units in the redoubt was ordered and building of permanent fortifications assigned to civilian construction companies. Intensive training was then started that took account of the continuously evaluated war experiences, so that by about 1943 Swiss fighting units were in the position to fulfill their assignments. During the dangerous summer of 1940, however, the Swiss army with few exceptions had not been ready for its task. From the start the will to resist was deeply rooted in the people and the army; but it was greatly shaken by the collapse of France and the obvious lack of the Swiss leadership's foresight. The spirit of resistance rebounded only slowly beginning in 1941, a development for which the section of the Swiss army called "Army and Home" created by General Guisan deserves great credit. With increasing combat readiness, the fighting spirit of the soldiers (which depended greatly on trust in their own ability and in that of their leaders) grew. In general, foreign observers accurately observed the gradual improvement of the Swiss instrument of defense. Yet it reached a level adequate to combat demands only in

---

[2]Chemical service, appendix to the report of the materials section on the active service of Sept. 25, 1945.

[3]Study on the final report on active service, BAR E 5795/310.

the last third of the war when the threat to Switzerland's continued existence had already diminished. Instead of just weeks, the army's build-up had consumed years.

Realistic Redoubt Concept

Secondly, the operative use of Switzerland's defensive instrument during the three main phases of the war shall be assessed. After the conclusion of Germany's Poland campaign and up to the looming collapse of France, a southern encirclement of France's defensive Maginot Line by the German Wehrmacht was a pre-eminent danger. General Guisan gave orders to barricade Switzerland's lowland region at the level of the river Limmat and to prepare the approaches to the back edges of the border for defensive delaying actions. The main line included the creation of strong continuous tank barriers, defended linearly from concrete bunkers. Invading troops would encounter a rear position along the valley ridge. Too little attention was paid to an immediate response by tactical reserves to local raids. The available forces were insufficient for a staggered deployment in greater depth. Possible breakthroughs by the enemy along the Reuss, the next continuous tank barrier, could therefore not be blocked.

Operative reserves were lacking. Particularly missing were armored vehicles for executing counterattacks to close breaches. A transition to mobile warfare was possible only in the pre-alpine region and the Jura. Due to the lack of equivalent units, a delaying action against a mechanized enemy between border regions and the Limmat also could not be undertaken with the desired vigor. The reinforced light infantry was only able to secure the prepared blastings and to make the rebuilding of destroyed targets more difficult. It would have been realistic to consider a combat strategy of delay. The German officers of the general staff who worked out the attack plans against Switzerland during the summer and fall of 1940 recognized the Swiss efforts to exact the highest price possible for a march through the country from the Northeast to the Northwest. They expected to have to fight a battle each along the border and in the Swiss lowlands and to have to fight for an approach to the Limmat. In the spring of 1940, however, the deterrent motives were irrelevant as the German leadership planned its offensive against France for geo-strategic reasons to start from the North through Luxemburg, Belgium and Holland. For a short time the possibility of a circumvention movement through Switzerland had been considered, but was rejected as offering no advantage. This decision may be attributed to the following reasons:

- Although the circumvention movement through Switzerland would threaten the economic and armament center of Lyon, it would lead to the strategic destination Paris only by detours and would not allow the separation of the British from the French forces.
- The disjointed Swiss terrain greatly limited the operations of mechanized units and gave the Swiss infantry many opportunities to block the few passages for a considerable time, so that no breakthroughs could be expected within a reasonable time.
- The fighting will of the Swiss people and the combat spirit of its army aroused the fear that resistance in the mountainous parts of the country could last for very long.

In 1940 neither the Swiss Federal Council nor the army command expected the collapse of France. They were totally surprised by this development and for all too long seemed unable to deal with it. For this reason decisive measures were taken only belatedly to adjust to the now-given threat of encirclement by a single power group. At the end of June and during July of 1940, therefore, when the danger was particularly acute, only a peripheral, thin, and easily breached defensive line was facing the attack contemplated by the German Führer. A large part of the Swiss population was resigned to confronting Hitler's invasion.

The partial retreat to the redoubt at the end of July 1940 spared at least half the army from being destroyed in the Swiss lowlands. In order to fully break the resistance, the attacker would also have been forced into a mountain war, which he wanted to avoid at all cost. But only by the pull-back of the whole army in the spring of 1941 to the central mountainous regions of Switzerland where enemy tanks and airplanes would have been hard pressed to deploy their might, was the new situation fully taken into account. The realistic concept of the redoubt created new confidence and formed the basis for overcoming the lowered morale. The concept was at first successfully kept secret from the Axis powers. In order to achieve its maximum dissuasive effect, it would perhaps have been better to present the idea on which the defense of Switzerland's central region was based, openly from the start. After all, the Germans feared nothing more than a mountain war of long duration and a lasting destruction of the Alpine transit routes. However, the latter threat had already been largely in place since July 1940. But the redoubt could unfold its force of deterrence only around the turn of the year 1940/41 after the Germans had recognized that the Swiss army was centered in the Alps.[4]

The Threat of a Long Defensive War

A study of Hitler's nervous ailment concludes that the German Führer's symptoms of illness appeared only in 1941; it observes, however, that as to character traits he was "emotionally labile, explosive, easily irritable in the sense of bad moods, and averse to making decisions".[5] Much angered by air incidents as well as by blunt statements in the Swiss press, and very disappointed by the failure of the Italian-German offensive in the Western Alps, in the summer of 1940 Hitler considered a punitive action against Switzerland and ordered appropriate preparations. Conciliatory gestures by the Federal Council relieved him of the necessity to actually execute the threats expressed in his protest memo. With his hesitancy in making decisions, he postponed the attack against the Swiss Confederation and finally dropped the idea. This allowed him to consider again matters of overall strategy in which Operation Switzerland had no priority.

After an expected final German victory, the country would simply have fallen without any further efforts into the lap of the Third Reich. It also would have been less necessary to take the Italian ally into consideration. The planned elimination of England as a war party, furthermore, and the later planned attack against Russia were not to be

---

[4]The opinion of P. Marguerat in *La Suisse face au IIIe Reich* [Switzerland Facing the Third Reich], p. 165ff, that the three meeting decision of July 1940 did not have a dissuasive effect has to be corrected accordingly.

[5]Ellen Gibbels, *Hitlers Nervenkrankheit* [Hitler's Neurosis], Quarterly Journal for Contemporary History, second issue.

endangered by fringe actions. Hitler also had to demonstrate his readiness to offer his hand for a peaceful solution in the West. An invasion of neutral Switzerland would have had the opposite effect. The protective shield that General Guisan hastily constructed towards the West was sparsely staffed, but relied on the strong terrain of the Jura as well as the deeply carved ditches of the Mentue and Paudèze regions. Towards the East, the army defended itself along the built-up Limmat position. The overall disposition was vulnerable.

In view of the hopeless strategic position of Switzerland, Hitler's military advisors counted on a rapid capitulation by the Federal Council. If that expectation would not be fulfilled or the army would continue to fight contrary to the wishes of the Federal Government, the Axis powers had to consider that the destruction of the defense potential, which for a small country was still quite formidable, might cause some real and prolonged trouble. The readiness of the Swiss soldiers to put a high price on their own heads meant that stiff defensive action had to be expected in strong and fortified areas of the country. It also could not be ruled out that individual, well-led Federal units would be able to retreat into mountainous regions and dig in for a lasting and grim struggle. This would tie down and use up German divisions that were needed elsewhere. If the Swiss defensive capacity had been weaker, Hitler and his generals would have been less hesitant to take advantage of favorable circumstances.

New Dangers after Turning
Fortunes of War 1942-43

Starting in 1941, the actions of the war moved away from Switzerland's borders. The German troops were fully engaged in the wide plains of Russia and the area of the Mediterranean. There were no forces to spare for side operations. After the turn in the fortunes of war during the winter of 1942/43, the discussions within the circles of the German general staff included a strategic retreat to "Fortress Europe". Those who favored this solution were hoping for the creation of strategic reserves by the retraction of the front which would permit the establishment of defensive centers and the conduct of counter-offensives. As Switzerland would be a natural component of "Fortress Europe", the

German leadership had to consider whether it could assume that the Federal Council and the Swiss army had the will and the power to independently defend its terrain against the Allies. However, for reasons of prestige Hitler never accepted the suggestions of his advisors, and ordered a tough defense of every square yard of occupied territory.

After 1943, the provisioning of the war in Italy increased the importance of the Swiss transit routes, so that extortion demands or even a forced attempt to bring the rail lines undamaged into German possession had to be expected. Due to operative discharges and an increased draft of able-bodied men, the Wehrmacht was able to keep a sizable number of units in reserve. Size and composition changed frequently. But it could not be ruled out that they might have been strong enough for a time to attack Switzerland. Such an event would have been even more dangerous, as on average only a scant quarter of the Swiss combat troops were on relief duty. For financial and economic reasons this was all that was possible. These troops of about 100,000 men had the task of warding off a first assault and making possible the remobilization of the main body of the army. Their task would have been difficult, as most of the remobilized soldiers had to get from their residences (which were outside of the central mountain regions) into the redoubt positions in order to take up the fight within the framework of their unit. It is questionable that the Swiss intelligence service would have been able to recognize enemy preparations early enough to be able to complete this delicate maneuver before an attack. At any rate, whatever was humanly possible was done in order not to be taken by surprise. Occasional dissuasive messages were designed to impress the incalculable risks of an attack upon the enemy.

After the opening of the second front in France, soon there were again battles along the Swiss border. After a while it became clear that the opposing enemy forces did not have enough troops to plan an operative detour across Swiss territory. However, tactical outflanking or retreats across Swiss terrain were certainly under consideration. The deployment of a suitable number of Swiss troops in the respective endangered border areas dampened such plans. Great efforts were also made to mark the border and to establish continuous contact with the parties at war.

Apart from the summer of 1940, when the drastic measures called for by the defeat of France were initiated a month and a half too late, it can be stated that Swiss operative decisions were taken and executed as demanded by a given situation and time. They maximized Switzerland's defensive possibilities and made occasional desires for conquest that were especially prevalent in German party circles appear unrealistic. Given Germany's difficult overall situation after the turn of the fortunes of war, an Operation Switzerland would have engaged too many forces for too long a time.

The Impact of Diplomacy

Diplomatic efforts contributed to defusing the situation. The speech given by the President of the Federal Council on June 25, 1940 which signaled a certain readiness to accommodate, and was followed by concessions in the matter of the air incidents, may have given Hitler the presumably welcome excuse to refrain from the threatened punitive expedition. While the President of the Federal Council Pilet-Golaz attempted to relax relations between Germany and Switzerland by his actions and discussions with the German Ambassador Köcher, General Guisan testified to the unbroken will of the army to resist in his Rütli report of July 25, 1940 as well as in his orders of the day. The various roles assumed by the Federal Government and the Supreme Commander of the Army in the disputes with the Third Reich ultimately complemented each other rather favorably. The German discovery of documents about the agreement between the French and Swiss High Command shook for a while the German Government's trust in the neutral stance of General Guisan, even though the planned military cooperation was based on an attack by Germany on Switzerland. They could have served to justify a preventive conquest of Switzerland. However, during politically sensitive talks with Schellenberg, General Guisan was able to eliminate the doubts about him and to strengthen the assumption that he would also most energetically fight off a possible American attack on Switzerland. While Great Britain showed a great deal of understanding for the Swiss situation and the Swiss point of view, the United States did the opposite. It may be questioned whether the Federal Department of Foreign Affairs had done all it could to bring about a change in the American attitude. Only in the spring of 1945 was it possible to conclude a somewhat satisfactory agreement.

Economic Measures

Just as important for the preservation of independence (as the generally smart diplomatic moves that accompanied military defense readiness) were the economic measures taken by the Federal Department of Economic Affairs in the context of the war.[6] The measures taken to protect and promote the domestic economy covered the following areas:

- Encourage keeping provisions by importers, companies and private households
- Increase production of domestic food production (Wahlen plan) and industrial products (by the use of substitute materials)
- Continue international trade
- Uniform and just distribution of scarce resources
- Foster employment in spite of lack of raw materials
- Avoid social emergencies by use of price and wage controls as well as by introducing wage and income replacement directives

The central office for the economy in wartime adopted the following priorities:

- Improve military preparedness and defense capability
- Maintain life, health and productivity of the civilian population
- Secure earnings and work possibilities
- Take special efforts to explain to the people the measures taken

Economic warfare, as opposed to military warfare, affected the neutral countries much harder than the nations at war. Although Switzerland was able to increase its imports during the first eight months of the war, by the summer of 1940 they dropped off significantly, as the measures of blockade and counter-blockade started to be felt, and Switzerland was largely at the mercy of the powers at war that surrounded its territory. The representatives of the commercial section opposed attempts to incorporate Switzerland into the blockade front

---

[6]The Swiss Wartime Economy 1939-1948.

with all available means and promoted the continuation of diplomatic relations with all sides. This was not easy. Negotiators offered the supply capability of Switzerland and its transport possibilities as bargaining chips for the use of seaports, the transit of goods, and supplies of indispensable raw materials. They played as their principal trump card Swiss capital strength. They gained thereby German permission for the shipment of goods important to the war economy through Axis controlled areas to and from countries in the West. During World War II, Switzerland obtained goods valued at 7.1 billion francs from Axis controlled areas and the neutral countries in Europe. In return it shipped goods valued at 5.3 billion francs to these countries. Swiss imports exceeded exports in quantity and value even in the trade with the Axis countries. This produced a negative balance for the Axis powers, which already suffered from a scarcity of goods.

The importance of Switzerland's shipment of war materials to the Third Reich is often generally exaggerated by researchers. Between 1940 and 1945, Switzerland exported products valued at 2.5 billion Swiss francs to Germany. Of this, only 600 million francs were actual war materials and 750 million francs were so-called strategic goods such as manufactured and semi-finished goods which were used by the weapons production industry. Together they accounted for only 0.6 percent (and war material as such only for 0.3 percent) of the total armament production of the Third Reich. Admittedly, they were for the most part specialty components and their lack would have impaired the production programs for tanks, aircraft, and remote control weapons. In addition, Switzerland financed its deliveries by clearing advances. By the end of the war these amounted to 1.1 billion francs. This concession was necessary in order to assure German deliveries of coal and iron, seeds, fertilizers, chemicals, mineral oil, and construction materials. Without this, it would have been impossible to expand agriculture, to maintain the level of employment, and to bring the army build-up to a satisfactory level. It was simply a question of survival.

After September 1939, Switzerland tolerated the unrestricted supply of war materials to both the Axis powers and the Allies. The country cannot be accused of having made a mistake, and even less of having violated neutrality when exports did not divide evenly. Already before the war, trade volume with Germany was about twice as large as that with Great Britain and the United States combined. During the war, imports from Allied countries nevertheless reached 2 billion Swiss francs and exports 1.7 billion francs. Under American leadership, the Allies started in 1942 to exert strong pressure on Switzerland by the establishment of blacklists and the refusal to provide urgently needed strategic materials. They demanded the cessation of clearing advances, a halt or at least a substantial reduction of the exports to Germany and of the transports on the Alpine transit routes. The Allies even considered a forced interruption of the Gotthard line, although on Italian soil. The success of this policy first became apparent in 1943. As of September 1944, Switzerland decreed a prohibition of the supply of war materials to all countries at war. It also increasingly reduced the transit traffic.[7]

More important than the delivery of war materials on credit to Germany were the purchases of German gold for Swiss francs by the National Bank. These purchases reached 1.2-1.3 billion francs. This hard currency enabled Germany to obtain its supplies on the world market. However, the National Bank also purchased gold from the Allies in the amount of more than 2 billion francs, which approximately equals the gold purchases from and clearing advances to Germany. [According to re-calculations of the Swiss National Bank, it purchased from Germany gold valued at 1,210 million francs between 1939 and 1945, from the Allies gold valued at a maximum of 1,940 million francs; see NZZ March 21, 1997.] The blemish remains that the German gold was for the most part so-called looted gold. It remains a controversial question if those responsible were aware of this fact.[8]

Switzerland's Use to Germany

Starting in the spring of 1940, the German leadership became aware of the importance of Switzerland's defense economy and of the Alpine transit routes. German leaders held two contradictory opinions. According to one view the most important thing was to suppress delivery of Swiss war materials to the Allies, according to the other view it was to increase the use of the Swiss armament industry for German purposes. The question remained open if these goals were best attained

---

[7]Marguerat, *La Suisse face au IIIe Reich*, particularly p. 94ff.
[8]Ibid, p. 120ff.

by a forced annexation of Switzerland or by political and economic pressures. During the summer of 1940, economic reasons were apparently not the determining factor in halting attack preparations.

During the following years, the war-related advantages provided by an independent Switzerland to Germany gained in importance. While the German armament centers suffered from bombardment, the Swiss industry was able to produce at full capacity. Quantitatively Swiss deliveries to Germany were not of great importance, yet they supplied mainly key components without which certain armament programs would have been drastically reduced. Electrical energy from Switzerland compensated for power failures in Southern Germany. However, the credits granted by Switzerland proved to be particularly important to the German war economy, as did the ability to exchange gold for Swiss currency, which enjoyed a good exchange rate on the world market. While the Austrian and French Alpine passes were often subject to air raids, the Gotthard and Simplon lines operated without disruption. Although no transports of troops or war material were permitted, the heavy coal transports relieved the remaining Alpine transit routes and made the continuation of the Italian armament production possible. All these advantages would have been lost by a forced action against Switzerland, as Swiss soldiers would have thoroughly destroyed the Alpine rail lines and as agents of the territorial army would have made those industries unusable and would have destroyed those goods which would have been of use to the enemy in the pursuit of war. The Swiss gold reserves for the most part had already been transferred overseas or were safely stored in the redoubt.

Switzerland offered certain advantages to all warring parties by taking on the diplomatic representation of their interests, by taking care of prisoners of war, by the efforts of the International Committee of the Red Cross, a purely Swiss institution, by providing humanitarian services such as the exchange of severely wounded soldiers, the housing of the severely ill and those in need of recuperation, and by alleviating pain and suffering abroad. Of particular importance, however, was its role as an international intelligence center. These services were particularly valued by the British, but to a certain extent also by the Germans. The least appreciative were the Americans, although they had established a first-rate espionage and intelligence-gathering bureau in Switzerland. They did not, however, consider risking these advantages by taking violent actions against Switzerland, such as the bombing of the Alpine transit routes.

No Power Vacuum

Swiss independence remained untouched during World War II primarily for reasons of strategic circumstances. An attack by Germany was not made at first, and later was no longer considered advisable. This opportunity would have been evaluated differently if there had been a power vacuum in Switzerland due to a lack of domestic stability or a lack of defensive power. However, this was not the case. Even during the summer of 1940 an attack on the Swiss Confederation could not be regarded as a cakewalk. In spite of the weakness of the Swiss army's defense arrangements, the German planners expected a tough fight. The rather deft Swiss diplomacy presented Hitler a chance to renounce the contemplated attack without loss of prestige and to give priority to considerations of opportunity. Switzerland's hour had not yet come. During the following years, Switzerland's increasing military prepared-ness forced the German Wehrmacht more and more to give it serious consideration. Eventually, the economic services and the good offices of an undamaged Switzerland were also taken into account. All forms of a state's activity play a role in total warfare. Depending on the situation, they could attract or repel the potential enemy. This effect was apparent even though the various domains had not yet been combined into a comprehensive plan of defense and had not been coordinated by a political strategy that focused on security.[9]

---

[9]Hans Senn, "Schweizerische Dissusionsstratgie im Zweiten Weltkrieg" [Swiss Dissuasion Strategy during World War II] in: *Schwedische und schweizerische Neutralität* [Swedish and Swiss Neutrality]; *Revue d'histoire de la deuxième Guerre mondiale*, January 1981.

IV: WHO PROLONGED THE SECOND WORLD WAR?

Walther Hofer

At least one member of the Bergier Commission, established by Switzerland's Federal Government, has proposed that further historical research be done to examine Jean Ziegler's absurd and provocative thesis that Switzerland prolonged the Second World War by some years and thus has the death of millions on its conscience. Jacob Tanner has put forward the view that, while Switzerland's contribution to the Nazi war effort was quantitatively very small, the matter looks quite differently when measured qualitatively. In his view, Switzerland facilitated the Nazi's procurement of strategic war materials on the world market, which was "a very decisive factor," so that, according to Tanner, one must at least "start with the hypothesis of a prolongation of the war, at least for now."

But this, notes the historian, must be followed by another step, an examination of factors "which contributed to the prolongation of the war, over which Switzerland had no influence." What he means here is Allied military strategy. Perhaps, Tanner continues, it would then emerge that the Swiss contribution was irrelevant compared to other factors. Taken as a whole, despite certain reservations, this line of reasoning seems to me worth examining (see *Basler Zeitung*, 21 May, 1995).

Financial Transactions and Exports

The observation that Swiss financial transactions in the final phase of the war could hardly have affected the duration of the conflict can be accepted – assuming that Swiss financial transactions and arms deliveries could have resulted in the prolongation of the war *at all*, which I seriously doubt, considering the proportions and quantities involved. If Swiss arms deliveries to wartime Germany were indeed worth 600 million francs, as recent calculations have shown, and if total German war costs were 1.2 trillion francs, as indicated by equally

76

reliable estimates, then Swiss arms deliveries amounted to a minuscule 0.05% of the total. Even if we amplify that by a factor of 10, the result is still only 0.5%. But the question of whether half of one percent could have prolonged the war cannot be answered at all. Indeed all such number games seem pointless. It will never be possible to reach any clear conclusions in this way, simply because there are too many imponderables in the picture.

That last observation also applies to the hard currency made available to Germany at that time. Prof. Jean-Claude Favez has already noted that a loss of its supply of Swiss francs – ostensibly so important to Germany according to some critics – would by no means necessarily have led, as suggested, to the end of Hitler's ability to wage war, since the German dictator had other possibilities open to him – including an invasion of Switzerland in order to seize a treasure in gold by force (*pace* Napoleon in 1798!). It should also be kept in mind that Germany remained quite capable of waging war – including the Ardennes offensive and the occupation of Hungary – for fully eight months after August-September 1944, when it was cut off from all foreign sources of assistance and thus unable to buy anything for whatever Swiss francs it may have gotten its hands on.

In his book *Die deutsche Wirtschaft 1930-45* [*The German Economy 1930-45,* p. 296] German economic historian Willi A. Boeckle raises the hypothetical question of what might have happened in 1943, for example, "if the Allies and the neutrals would have suddenly cut off all their exports of vital raw materials to Germany? Would the Second World War then have ended as suddenly as it had begun?" And he responds: "[These are] questions to which there are many answers." It is evident that Ziegler erroneously cites Boeckle to support his untenable premise that the war would have ended in two months if the flow of Swiss francs to Germany had been halted.

Also of interest in this context are some comments made by Albert Speer in his memoirs [cf. Speer, *Erinnerungen* (Berlin 1969), p. 329]. He was, in effect, Germany's munitions czar, and succeeded in bringing German arms production to its highest levels as late as July 1944. In a memorandum to Hitler dated December 1943, Speer stresses Germany's serious shortages of metal alloys. Germany was almost totally dependent on imports for its manganese ore, bauxite and chromium; the worst bottleneck was in the supply of chromium, of which Turkey was the most important supplier. And so Speer concluded that the war would end about 10 months after the loss of the Balkans – which is just what happened. Yet Speer does not even mention Switzerland in his calculations.

The Pre-War Role of the Big Powers

It is almost an imposition to have to deal, against all reason, with the exaggeration of little Switzerland into an imagined factor of such magnitude that it could have decided the duration of World War II. It was primarily, if not exclusively, the Great Powers who did so. Which brings us to Jacob Tanner's "third step."

It was largely due to the Big Powers that Switzerland found itself in such a difficult situation in the years after 1940: mainly Germany, because it deliberately caused the war; Italy, because it let itself be dragged along in Hitler's wake; the Soviet Union, because with the Hitler-Stalin Pact it gave the green light for Germany's invasion of Poland; France and England – and the USA – because they allowed Hitler's policy of aggression to go on for all too long, or else tried to counter it with the wrong methods.

Those who are unwilling to see this historical context as a whole are taking a superficial view. In my own academic studies on this subject I have consistently stressed that the series of victories chalked up by the Wehrmacht was by no means due only to German competence and Hitler's qualities as a military commander; equally responsible were the unsuccessful, not to say catastrophic, policies and strategies of his opponents. With regard to England, the former U.S. ambassador to Switzerland, Faith Whittlesey, speaks of Neville Chamberlain's "insane actions" (cf. *Der Bund*, 31 May 1977), by which she obviously means the prewar prime minister's policy of appeasement. Then there was the utter failure of France's policy and strategy toward Nazi expansionism – e.g. in the case of the remilitarization of the Rhineland in 1936, when an energetic reaction, at more or less minimal risk and cost, might well have nipped the war in the bud.

How different was the reaction of even so "simple" a man as Rudolf Minger, then head of the Swiss Department of the Military. Having predicted Hitler's march into the Rhineland in January 1936, after that event he wrote that Germany was not yet ready for a war of aggression, and it was an open question how much longer it would take. Then came the truly prophetic statement: "In my opinion we have to reckon on about three years." – i.e., 1939! [cf. Walther Hofer, "Neutraler Kleinstaat im europäischen Konfliktfeld," in *Kriegsausbruch 1939*, ed. Altrichter and Becker (Munich 1989), p. 317].

If only the leaders of the major Western powers had had such foresight! There was, of course, Winston Churchill, but he was a voice crying in the wilderness, in sharp opposition to official government policy of the time. In February 1938 Chamberlain let the smaller European countries know that they could not count on the League of Nations' assistance in the event of conflict – a clear declaration of moral bankruptcy. Whereupon Switzerland announced its return to a policy of "integral (or full) neutrality."

Anyone attempting to judge the operation of Swiss neutrality during World War II should first take all these facts into account. If, after the unexpected collapse of France in 1940, Switzerland found itself caught in a very awkward position, it was hardly the fault of the Swiss. On the contrary, they were victims of international developments upon the course of which they had not the slightest influence.

American policy during those prewar years was also anything but helpful. As President Franklin D. Roosevelt himself later declared, the "neutrality legislation" which was to guide U.S. foreign policy from 1935 onward only served to encourage the aggressors – Italy in Ethiopia, Japan in China, Germany in Europe. Walter Lippmann, the prominent American news analyst, was even more sarcastic in his evaluation, declaring that such a policy has "attained the brink of absurdity and total bankruptcy."

Recalling this American self-criticism today alters nothing in our acknowledgment of America's subsequent commitment in the struggle against the aggressors. The Swiss are fully aware that the Allied victory also saved their own freedom and independence. But that should not lead to denying the fact that the Second World War could, in all probability, have been avoided if the United States, as the most powerful nation in the Free World, had thrown its weight into the scales of global politics early enough, as it did in 1945 in order to prevent the Bolshevization of Europe.

It is far from pleasant for us to pass judgment on the mistakes of governments and peoples who ultimately, at great sacrifice and horrible loss of life, defeated the aggressors. But today, with Switzerland being judged and condemned by some in a highly questionable and one-sided manner, it is time to recall the sins of others as well.

The balance is especially equivocal in the case of the former Soviet Union. The people under Stalin's rule certainly paid the heaviest price in blood, and for this we continue to owe them the profoundest gratitude. But that cannot obscure the evil role which the Soviet dictator played in the making of the Second World War. He not only prolonged the war, he made it possible in the first place. I noted this in my book *Die Entfesselung des Zweiten Weltkriegs [Unleashing the Second World War]* published more than forty years ago, which brought me the criticism that I was an anti-Soviet historian. But after the collapse of Communism, the fact was confirmed by the Russian historian Vyachislav I. Dashichev, who wrote that Stalin had made it possible for Hitler "to unleash World War II under the most favorable conditions" (cf. Knopp und Schott, *Die Saat des Krieges [The Seeds of War]*. Bergisch Gladbach, 1989, p. 317). Those "favorable conditions" were the USSR's strategic cover for Hitler's campaigns against Western Europe and Moscow's deliveries to Germany of the necessary raw materials and foodstuffs.

According to the standard text issued by the Office of Military History Research in Freiburg im Breisgau, *Das deutsche Reich und der Zweite Weltkrieg [The German Reich and the Second World War]*, the Soviet Union supported Hitler Germany "to a high degree" with political propaganda and, even more, with economic assistance. The figures provided by that source are indeed huge: 1 million tons of oil; 800,000 tons of iron ore; 500,000 tons of phosphates; 100,000 tons of chromium ore (!); 80,000 tons of manganese; 10,8000 tons of copper; 1,575 tons of nickel; 13,000 tons of rubber; 985 tons of tin, etc. etc., plus 2.22 million tons of grain. Vyacheslav M. Molotov, then the Soviet foreign minister and architect of the notorious Hitler-Stalin pact, openly remarked more than once that Soviet supplies had been "not without influence on the great German victories." And the German author of the relevant article in *Das deutsche Reich und der Zweite Weltkrieg* states: "Of vital importance for Germany until 1941 was the fact that the Soviet Union shipped to the Reich large quantities of a broad range of raw materials it lacked, rendering [Germany] capable of conducting a long war of attrition against the Western powers" (cf. Vol. IV, pp. 89 ff.). And Hitler gloated that those Soviet deliveries completely thwarted the British blockade.

It was not the Swiss banks and anonymous Swiss "fences" who financed Hitler's war of aggression; it was Stalin who made it possible. Ultimately, in one of fate's ironies, it was also the Soviet dictator who made possible Hitler's war against his own country. Summing up, it may be said that Stalin had the chance to prevent the war entirely, but instead chose to give Hitler the opportunity of plunging Western Europe into a bloodbath.

Allied Strategies and Policies

In the search for reasons why the war was prolonged, certain strategic and policy decisions in the Western Allies' conduct of the war should not be overlooked. Let us limit ourselves here to examining two such miscalculations.

The first case involves the war in the Mediterranean, and especially in Italy. After the surprising downfall of Mussolini in July 1943 – by which time the Allies had already landed in Sicily – it was the clearly expressed desire of the successor regime under Marshal Badoglio to bring Italy into the Allied camp as quickly as possible and get rid of the Germans with equal dispatch. For a time, the Allies had a chance to occupy Italy more or less without a fight, in conjunction with the Italian army. But, bound by the formula of "unconditional surrender," they let valuable time pass, which Hitler promptly used to occupy Italy himself. (Incidentally, that German blitz goes some way to negate the assertion contained in the Eizenstat Report that the Wehrmacht no longer constituted any danger to Switzerland after 1943.)

As to that disastrous formula of "unconditional surrender", in his book *The Second World War* (1948, pp. 264 ff), the noted British military historian J.F.C. Fuller remarks somewhat sarcastically that there was "a wrangle" between the representatives of Badoglio and Eisenhower over the interpretation of those two words. "Under cover of this causistry," he observes, "the Germans poured fourteen divisions into Italy." And further: "This foolishness conceived by President Roosevelt and Mr. Churchill at Casablanca trapped the British and Americans into tactically the most absurd and strategically the most senseless campaign of the whole war." The unfortunate phrase, Fuller maintains, turned Germany's "soft underbelly" into a crocodile's back, prolonged the war, devastated Italy and cost thousands of British and American lives (as well as those of soldiers from many other nations, including Poles who fought at Monte Casino – which may also serve as a sad symbol of this entire ruinous campaign).

The importance which a swift liberation of Italy would have had for Switzerland may be gauged from the fact that the country would have been freed from German encirclement an entire year sooner – quite aside from the enormous strategic advantages which would have accrued to the Western Allies in their race with the Russians to liberate Southeast and Central Europe. Though a push in that direction would have accorded with Churchill's deepest desires, in his memoirs oddly enough he maintains that he does not believe this operational possibility could have been foiled by the insistence on unconditional surrender.

The second case we shall examine here involves the Western Allies' strategy in the final phase of the war, specifically in the autumn of 1944. Following the blitzkrieg-like conquest of all of France, General Eisenhower, the Supreme Allied Commander, halted his huge invading army near the German and Belgian frontiers in August-September of that year, claiming supply line problems as the main reason. Britain's Field Marshall Montgomery, on the other hand, proposed that all supply lines be concentrated on one army – preferably his own – and that the war be brought to an end with a powerful push into Germany. But Eisenhower held to his own strategy of advancing on a broad front. By the time he yielded and gave Montgomery a green light, it was "a month too late," in the words of Chester Wilmot in his standard work *The Struggle for Europe* (New York: Harper, 1952. – German translation: *Der Kampf um Europa*. Zürich 1954, pp. 557 ff.). By that time, the once crumbling German front had somewhat solidified once again.

It is also the opinion of many other authoritative military experts that a strong push with an army of about 15 divisions, executed early enough, would either have ended the war quickly or at least shortened it by months. Particularly important is the view of German commanders in this matter. Chester Wilmot summarizes the opinions of von Rundstedt, Westphal, Blumentritt, Speidel and others in these words: "...

in September [1944] a concentrated thrust from Belgium would have led to success" – specifically the conquest of the lower Rhineland and, even more important, the Ruhr District. In any case, this would have meant that Hitler could no longer have launched the Ardennes offensive which gave the Allies so much trouble.

In his work *Der Zweite Weltkrieg: Kriegsziele und Strategie der grossen Mächte [The Second World War: Objectives and Strategy of the Great Powers,* 1983), German military historian Andreas Hillgruber notes that, given the miserable state of Germany's Western Army (which Eisenhower's staff obviously failed to realize), the leading Wehrmacht commanders "reckoned with the collapse of the Reich in August-September 1944" (p. 139) if the enemy [i.e. the Allies] had continued its advance. And J.F.C. Fuller, referring to Montgomery's plan, says succinctly: "And we think that the verdict of history will be that he was right." (p. 339).

I want to stress once more that I am not concerned here with casting aspersions on those to whom we ultimately owe the glorious victory over Hitler's Wehrmacht. But when Switzerland is being accused of having contributed to prolonging the war, then it is the historians' right, indeed their duty, to place that accusation into the general context of strategic decisions and miscalculations. From the perspectives sketched here, it seems obvious that speculation about a Swiss contribution to the prolongation of the Second World War seems idle and virtually irrelevant.

PART THREE

POLITICS

V: NEUTRAL SWITZERLAND –
HUMANITARIAN SWITZERLAND:

A Contradiction?

Hugo Bütler

To commemorate Switzerland's survival during World War II and the role it played in those years, but particularly in connection with the 150th anniversary of the founding of modern Switzerland, the Swiss Federal Council proposed in 1998 to set up a large solidarity fund which, as a work of the century, would reach far into the future. For this purpose the gold reserves of the National Bank are to be re-appraised and half the appreciated value used to create, step by step, a foundation capital of seven billion francs. Of the estimated annual yield of 300 to 400 million francs, half would be used at home and half abroad to aid people in need. In a non-bureaucratic way support is to be given to victims of catastrophes, poverty, genocide, torture, wars, and violations of human rights.

A solidarity fund of this type would reinforce and revitalize Switzerland's humanitarian tradition. The latter began long before 1859/1864 with the failed Geneva banker Henri Dunant's idea of the Red Cross after his visit to the battle of Solferino. For instance, after the reformation, Switzerland already had offered a haven to victims of religious warfare and French absolutism and later to those persecuted and victimized by the European political revolutions. Whether Switzerland did enough and all that was possible at the time for those threatened and outcast by Hitler's barbarism has been the subject of critical discussion for some time and remains the theme of new reflections. These should be maintained, if only for reasons of human conscience, when one considers the "Jew stamps" in passports and refugees turned back at the borders, which often led to their demise in Hitler's death camps. It is possible that comparisons with other countries will show that Switzerland, greatly threatened as it was, achieved relatively much in the refugee drama of the Hitler years. However failures occurred here as well as there.

Immediately after the war, the idea of "solidarity" emerged as a guiding principle of Switzerland's policy towards the world and as a mark of openness that is to accompany Swiss neutrality and benevolence. Apart from negotiations and the payment of 250 million Swiss francs within the framework of the Washington agreement of 1946, it took concrete form in the Swiss Donation to War Victims. When the fund raising was completed in 1948 almost 206 million francs in aid were contributed from public sources and large sums collected from the people; in today's value this would be about one billion francs. Since the 1950s, large sums are also contributed annually from the government's treasury as well as from citizens, to go for development and assistance projects in Third World countries. The traditional humanitarian organization of Switzerland, the International Committee of the Red Cross, the ICRC, receives apart from considerable private donations more that 100 million francs annually from public funds; other countries also pay annually several hundred million francs in support of the ICRC's fieldwork.

These numbers and their magnitude show that the Swiss approach to solidarity will not and should not now or in the future be guided by a hard-hearted or stingy mentality in the encounter with human suffering and dire need. The foundation capital of the envisaged new Swiss Solidarity Fund is of such a scope that it can take its rightful place alongside other large and worldwide humanitarian efforts. As there will be sufficient resources to use only the annual proceeds without touching the capital itself, the Fund promises a degree of effectiveness that will thoroughly outdistance the controversies generated by the shadows that cloud Swiss actions during World War II. Responsible management of the Fund and a well thought out utilization of its proceeds (which actually belong to Switzerland's people, but do not come from their tax payment), are a precondition of the Fund's success.

As the debate about the Swiss role during World War II highlights, the armed neutrality of the Swiss confederation has been and still is considered suspect by critics within and without the country. According to a simplistic, moralizing point of view of these critics, Switzerland had wrongly decided not to join the warring party of the Allies and their blockade against Hitler's Germany. As did other neutral countries, it maintained instead commercial and financial relations with the "enemy" to the end, thus benefitting Hitler and his war economy. In short, the

Swiss attitude was and still remains basically suspect to the black-and-white mentality of these people. In the opinion of former U.S. Senator D'Amato, who appears unwilling to learn anything new, Switzerland had not been neutral, but had "fully collaborated" with Hitler's Germany.

This attitude is similar to how the American victors in the fight against Hitler's dictatorship saw the Swiss Confederation in 1945 when they decided to admit only those countries to the newly organized United Nations that had declared war on Germany by March of that year. However, this untenable concept was dropped a few years later, and neutral countries such as Sweden and Austria were admitted to the UN.

Those who must wage war tend to adopt a friend-enemy attitude and easily adopt the false posture: "Those who are not for me, are against me." The idea of armed neutrality is highly complex and fully opposite to such thinking. It requires self-reliance, a desire to deliver the country to neither side of the warring parties, the maintenance of diplomatic and economic relations that are balanced towards both belligerents, and a threat of defensive warfare against anyone who attempts to disturb the independence and peace of the neutral country. Based on these demands to maintain the country's security and with the support of the major parties from left to right, the Swiss government pursued the goal of steering the nation between 1939 and 1945 unscathed through World War II. Switzerland's Federal Executive and Parliament reached this demanding goal with the support of a generation of dedicated Swiss women and men. Freedom, democracy, and the protection of some 300,000 refugees were assured, in spite of all restrictions and the fear-ridden isolation of a severely threatened country. Activities in favor of the National Socialists were punished; Swiss citizens who defected to the Nazis and joined the armed SS were put on trial.

It is undoubtedly to be expected that staying on the sidelines and maintaining neutrality during times of ruthless war led to friction and moral ambiguities, especially during the years of total encirclement by the Axis powers. The dealings of the Swiss National Bank (as well as by the Bank for International Settlements, BIS, located in Basel) with gold looted by the Germans from occupied countries are part of these ambiguities that require clarification and that today have led to a new understanding. However, would Switzerland in the end have better served its own interests and those of Europe's threatened people by surrendering its neutrality?

In 1938, little Austria showed more enthusiasm than reluctance in being "annexed", occupied and, finally, fully incorporated into Hitler's war machine. Those who speak today in the World War Two context of a "Waldheimization" of Switzerland reveal themselves as inventors of nonsense. Hitler ruthlessly overran weak Belgium, Denmark, and Norway. What saved Switzerland from occupation and war with the Germans were these factors: the spiritual and political will to resist, integral neutrality, defensive armed preparedness, economic exchange with both warring parties, negotiating skills, and luck. On the European continent Switzerland remained the last protector of freedom, the last refuge for a free German language theater, the last hope (often unfortunately also disappointment) of threatened refugees.

Was Swiss neutrality sustained at the expense of and to the disadvantage of the Allies in their war against Hitler? Would it have been desirable for the Allies (or for us) if they had also to liberate Switzerland from Hitler's henchmen? Let those who really believe this come forward. A free Switzerland was, after all, rather indispensable, not the least for the Allies' intelligence services. On November 29, 1943, the British General Staff explained in a memorandum to its American counterpart how Switzerland via the ICRC protected and cared for the prisoners of war and how useful it was in supplying precision instruments indispensable to Allied war technology, an activity for which the Swiss agents had wrested agreement from the Germans. The favorable judgment of Churchill, Hitler's most relentless enemy, is well known; it is also noteworthy that in 1946 he used Swiss soil to call upon Germany and France, recently enemies in war, to seek reconciliation and cooperation.

If Switzerland created an aid fund for victims of the Holocaust (1997) and proposes to establish a humanitarian solidarity fund for the new millennium, it does so not because it is ashamed of its neutrality during World War II. Quite the opposite: humanitarian efforts and neutrality are very much intertwined particularly during times of war. Limitations, our own as well as those of others, and suffering of people challenge us today as much as yesterday to mitigate pain and to help those in need. That should be motivation enough and ease the re-examination of our history.

VI: CONTESTED SWISS NEUTRALITY

Dietrich Schindler

Swiss neutrality in World War II has been severely criticized by U.S. Undersecretary of State Stuart E. Eizenstat in the Foreword to the Eizenstat Report[1]. Interestingly, however, the Foreword differs considerably from the main part of the Report. While the latter gives an objective description of the conduct of the Allies and the neutral states in World War II and in the postwar period, the Foreword contains political assessments which to a large. extent have no basis in the main part of the Report. The present article will examine the criticisms raised by Undersecretary Eizenstat about Swiss neutrality in World War II.

Immoral Neutrality?

Although the Foreword reminds us to be "cautious in making simplistic moral judgments about the conduct of neutral nations in wartime," such judgments do have a prominent position in it. One of them is the general statement that: "... in the unique circumstances of World War II, neutrality collided with morality; too often being neutral provided a pretext for avoiding moral considerations." Although this statement points to a real and serious problem, it qualifies neutrality from the outset as morally reprehensible. When one considers the situation of Switzerland in World War II, one has to realize that Switzerland had no choice other than to remain neutral. The Western Great Powers, the only ones which could have stopped Hitler's aggressive policy in time, tolerated his provocations for years (e.g. the occupation of the Rhineland in 1936) or expressly accepted them (e.g. the incorporation by Germany of the German-speaking parts of Czechoslovakia by the Munich agreement of 1938). They thereby encouraged him to adopt even more aggressive conduct. The League of

---

[1]Report by the Chief of the General Staff on the active service, Materials section.

Nations, whose task was to maintain international peace, failed because the Great Powers did not live up to their commitments. The United States, paralyzed by isolationism at the end of World War I, stayed out of it and thereby weakened it from the beginning. When Germany, Italy and Japan felt increasingly free to commit aggressions, many European countries reverted to a policy of strict neutrality believing that in doing so they could avoid being dragged into the coming war. The United States, in 1935, 1936 and 1937, amended its neutrality legislation in this sense, prohibiting arms exports, loans and credits to belligerent countries. The term "super-neutrality" was used in this connection. After the outbreak of the war, however, the United States reversed its policy and started assisting Britain and France. But only the Japanese attack on Pearl Harbor in December 1941 provoked its entry into the war.

Credibility versus Opportunism

Participation in the war was out of the question for Switzerland throughout the entire war unless it was itself attacked. Even when the German defeat was in sight and the Allies put pressure on the few remaining neutrals to give up neutrality and to declare war on the Axis powers, Switzerland never considered doing so. As it was surrounded by the Axis powers (and later on only by German forces), Germany would in all probability have reacted by occupying as much Swiss territory as possible. Besides that, neutrality had for centuries been a Swiss maxim, motivated by its geographical situation in the center of Great Powers, and deeply rooted in democratic convictions. It would have been impossible to make a sudden opportunistic turn when the tide of the battle shifted in the Allies' favor. Turkey and Argentina had fewer problems in this respect. Under Allied pressure they declared war on Germany in February and March 1945 and thereafter were admitted to the founding conference of the United Nations in San Francisco. By so doing, they avoided many of the problems which Switzerland went through after the end of the war. However, the question remains open whether they acted in better harmony with morality than Switzerland.

The fact that Switzerland refused to break off completely its trade with Germany even in March 1945 was not, as Eizenstat suggests, a pretext for making profits but resulted from the conviction that it had to continue to fulfill the duties incumbent on a neutral country in order to keep its credibility. In all matters in which the law of neutrality left freedom to the neutrals, Switzerland complied with Allied requests. When the Allied mission to Switzerland led by Lauchlin Currie, President Roosevelt's Administrative Assistant, ended its negotiations in March 1945, a communiqué stated: "...the Allied Governments manifested their full understanding of Switzerland's particular neutrality which they had always respected."

Prolonging the War?

Eizenstat is correct when he states that World War II was not just another war and also when he says: "Nazi Germany was a mortal threat to Western civilization itself and, had it been victorious, to the survival of even the neutral countries themselves." In fact. when a war is fought between a totalitarian state and a free democracy, Switzerland cannot but stand up for the cause of the free democracy. This was also true in the struggle between the free world and communist totalitarianism. This does not, however, mean that all states have to break off their relations with totalitarian states and go to war against them. As long as states cling to their sovereignty and are not ready to be integrated into a general security system, their conduct cannot be judged on the basis of one single principle. Rather, their individual situation must be taken into consideration.

Eizenstat's reproach that Switzerland prolonged the war is one of his further undifferentiated judgments. Undoubtedly, the supply of arms did not weaken Germany. But it must be emphasized – and this has not been known to the authors of the Eizenstat Report – that Switzerland during World War II imported five times more weapons and other war material from Germany for its own defense (to be used in case of a German attack) than it exported to Germany. When assessing the advantages and disadvantages Swiss neutrality had for the Allied cause, one must take into consideration the consequences which Switzerland's entry into the war would have had, notably including: the cessation of protection of prisoners of war, the cessation of humanitarian assistance to the victims of war, the cessation of the representation of US and British interests in Germany, the closing of the US intelligence center in Switzerland, the sequestration of all Swiss and Allied assets in Switzerland in case of occupation, the extermination of the Jewish population and Jewish refugees in Switzerland. A simplistic answer on the advantages and disadvantages of Swiss neutrality is hardly possible.

Problematic Sides of Swiss Neutrality: Arms Trade

The fact that Switzerland had no other choice than to remain neutral does not imply that it handled its neutrality impeccably in every respect. Its conduct shows positive and negative sides. First and foremost, Switzerland cannot be blamed for having based its neutrality on the law of neutrality, which had been codified in the two Hague Conventions on neutrality in 1907. This was the only safe basis to resist the claims of belligerents incompatible with neutrality, such as the German demand to restrict the freedom of the press. The law of neutrality enabled Switzerland to maintain trade with both belligerent sides during the entire duration of the war. Moreover, the law of neutrality permits private exports of arms to belligerents. Undoubtedly, this rule, taken as self-evident in the period of economic liberalism in which it was adopted, became problematic with the emergence of total warfare. Most states today regulate the arms trade. The distinction between admissible private trade and prohibited state trade has thereby become blurred since 1907. However, during World War II arms trading carried out by private enterprises was considered compatible with neutrality.

On April 14, 1939, the Swiss government prohibited arms exports to belligerent states, believing that this would enable it to conduct a morally incontestable neutrality in the coming war, but it changed its decision shortly after the outbreak of the war under pressure from France and Britain, which had for years neglected their own armaments. The Swiss government realized that Switzerland, lacking any raw materials, could not obtain goods for its survival without furnishing weapons in return. After the French defeat in 1940 and the encirclement of Switzerland by the Axis powers, arms were exported mainly to Germany, but Switzerland also managed to export some goods of military importance to the Allied countries even in this period. It may be added that the law of neutrality does not require equality of the volume of trade with both belligerents.

Although arms trading was legally permissible, the way it was carried out by Switzerland was not entirely up to legal standards. In the beginning, the government determined that arms could be exported only against cash payment or against goods essential for Switzerland's survival, but this principle was soon disregarded in favor of generous credits. Thus Germany could obtain arms on credit, which was not compatible with the law of neutrality.

Negligence in Other Fields

Established practice was also the cause of negligence in other fields. The acceptance of gold from the German Reichsbank by the Swiss National Bank was both usual and legally admissible, but routine made the responsible persons careless about the origin of the gold. Similarly, closing the borders was a measure in conformity with international law. Refugees had no right to be admitted nor was the prohibition of "refoulement", i.e. the prohibition to expel or return a refugee to territories where his life or freedom would be threatened on account of his race, nationality or similar status, part of international law at that time. The responsible persons' conviction to act in conformity with then-current law obscured their capacity to see the consequences of their conduct.

Moral and Political Isolation after the War

At the end of the war, the Swiss population was convinced that armed neutrality had saved it from being directly involved in the war, and it began to consider armed neutrality as a principle also to be followed in the future. The fact that it had been the Allied victory which had saved Switzerland from the totalitarian threat could not induce the government and the people to reconsider neutrality and to collaborate more actively in the reconstruction of a stable international order. The Allies reinforced this attitude by excluding from the founding conference of the United Nations all states which had not declared war against the Axis powers and by rejecting any form of neutrality in the framework of the UN. The defensive Swiss attitude was furthermore corroborated by the pressure exerted by the Allies to hand over to them the

German assets in Switzerland and the gold acquired from the German Reichsbank. Both claims were rejected as incompatible with international law. However, Switzerland was no longer placed between two belligerents which could be played off against each other but stood in front of a compact block of Allied states which made heavy demands on it. It found itself, as William E. Rappard remarked, in a moral and political isolation never before experienced in its history.

The Washington Accord of 1946

The Eizenstat Report deals extensively, both in its main part and in the Foreword, with the Allied-Swiss Accord signed in Washington on May 26, 1946. With respect to this point, too, the almost exclusively negative appreciation of the Swiss attitude in the Foreword contrasts with the objective description of the viewpoints of both sides in the main report. The rejection by Switzerland of the demand to hand over to the Allies all German assets in Switzerland, including those of Nazi victims, does not deserve the criticism given by Eizenstat but, on the contrary, a positive judgment. Handing over these assets amounted to confiscation without compensation, in violation of international law, and to recognition of a collective guilt of all Germans, including the victims of Nazism. The Swiss defended not only fundamental principles of international law but, in view of the indiscriminate treatment of Nazis and Nazi victims, fundamental principles of morality. When the Cold War started, however, the Allies gave up their attempt to prevent the economic recovery of Germany by confiscating German property.

On the other hand, Switzerland's behavior was not completely laudable. Internal pressure prevented it from defending German property rights to the very end. Many Swiss claimed that the German assets should be used to satisfy Swiss claims against Germany. The Washington negotiations ended in a compromise which addressed these claims. In the matter of the German gold, Switzerland based its position on the traditional right of Germany as an occupying power to seize state property of an occupied state in certain circumstances and on the good faith of the Swiss National Bank, while the Allies considered all acquisition of property by the occupying power as illegal. Although the Washington Accord did not constitute a complete defeat for Switzerland, it was considered as such in Switzerland. It was described as a "diktat", a "capitulation" and as "deepest humiliation".

The Cold War as Rescue for Switzerland's Neutrality

The Cold War forced the Allies to turn to other problems and thus to lessen pressure on Switzerland. Eizenstat observes that Switzerland was now seen as a democratic deterrent to Soviet expansionism. The East-West confrontation led to a renewed understanding of the principle of neutrality (not mentioned by Eizenstat), as was first shown by the 1953 Korean cease-fire agreement which set up two neutral commissions in which Switzerland participated. In 1955, Austria committed itself to "practice in perpetuity a neutrality of the type maintained by Switzerland". The new esteem for neutrality reinforced Switzerland's belief that its neutrality, as practiced in World War II, was the best policy to pursue. It did not see any need to adapt its policy to the changes brought about by World War II. The services of neutrals for war prevention, peacekeeping, and all kinds of "good offices" became increasingly sought after. Switzerland continued to perform such functions but, as most of them can now be accomplished in the framework of the United Nations, its respective activities remained rather limited due to its absence from the United Nations. It thereby missed an opportunity to show the positive sides of its neutrality and to win a better comprehension of it in the international community. Concentration on humanitarian aid, following Swiss tradition, remains important but cannot replace cooperation in other fields.

The end of the Cold War ended the privileged position of neutrals. Switzerland was now forced to assume a more active role in the international community and to intensify its cooperation on the multilateral level in order to remain a respected member of the international community. It adapted itself to the new situation insofar as it has taken part, without being a member of the UN, in all sanctions decided upon by the Security Council since the Iraq-Kuwait crisis of 1990. But in recent months, the moral and political isolation, which had been experienced in the postwar period, was suddenly felt again as a consequence of the campaign led against Switzerland because of its conduct in World War II. Switzerland is now forced simultaneously to solve problems which have remained unsolved in the past decades and to cope with the urgent problems of the present time such as its relations with the European Union and the United Nations. The cumulation of these problems and the fact that the Swiss people are sharply divided with respect to them makes the task particularly arduous.

VII: SWITZERLAND, INTERNATIONAL LAW AND WORLD WAR II

Detlev F. Vagts

The recent sudden upsurge of interest in Swiss behavior during and after World War II seems to call for a brief review of the international law issues that were relevant to that country's decisions. Many of them, in particular the law of neutrals, have become obsolete and are obviously not understood by many commentators. Of course, to reach a judgment that the behavior of Switzerland was compatible with the rules of international law which were then in effect does not dispose of issues of humanity and morality. But it does contribute to explaining Swiss behavior, particularly since the Government in Bern was quite legalistic in its approach to the questions of the time.

It has been remarked that, over time, the moral standing of neutrals has declined.[1] To have been neutral as between Germany and France in 1870-1871 or Russia and Japan in 1904-1905 was to stand aside from a quarrel that affected only those two parties and arguably should never have caused resort to arms. To remain neutral in 1914-1918 or 1939-1945 was to shrink from taking part in what the participants – amounting to a high proportion of the inhabitants of the globe – regarded as a crusade. Let it be remembered, however, that from 1914 to 1917 the United States was a neutral nation and tried, more or less, to conform to the rules of neutrality as understood at the time. In 1917 we then went to war, believing that our neutral rights had been intolerably abused by the kaiser.[2] From 1939 to 1941, the United States was again neutral, although such steps as the destroyer bases deal and lend-lease took us further and further away from the traditional rules of neutrality. In 1941 we were precipitated out of neutrality and into war, not through our own deliberate decision but by the Japanese attack on Pearl Harbor and the concomitant declarations of war by Japan and Germany.[3]

---

[1] Josef L. Kunz, *The Laws of War*, 50 AJIL 313, 326 (1956) (stating that "neutrality was looked upon as something immoral, if not criminal").

[2] Charles C. Tansill, *America Goes to War* (1938).

[3] For a review of neutrality practice in the period before Pearl Harbor, see Hans L. Trefousse, *Germany and American Neutrality, 1939-1941* (1951); the same events are seen in German perspective in Friedrich Berber, *Die*

As a culmination of the decline of neutrality came the advent of the United Nations. In that Organization it could be argued that such states as Eire and Portugal were not eligible for membership because they had not fought in World War II and hence did not meet the "peace-loving" standard.[4] Particularly devastating to neutrality was the grant of power to the Security Council to declare binding boycotts of offending nations, which means that there are hostilities in which nobody can be neutral. Nobody, that is, except Switzerland, which has never joined the United Nations. In effect, on such occasions as the Persian Gulf war, countries can be drafted into the service of the United Nations and compelled to interrupt communications and trade with the party designated as the offender, even though their armed forces cannot be conscripted to participate in the fighting. To be sure, there have been some episodes of serious fighting in which the Security Council has not acted – the struggle over the Malvinas/Falklands between Argentina and Britain and the long Iran/Iraq war come to mind – but the neutrality issues they generated were not highlighted.[5] Thus, it takes an act of historical reconstruction to understand the concepts of neutrality that were part of the framework within which states made decisions from 1939 to 1945.

First, the neutrality of Switzerland had a rather special basis in international law. It was not merely that the country chose to remain neutral but, rather, that there was an international understanding that it should remain so. At one time Switzerland was a warlike country involved in repeated combat with its neighbors. Its soldiers were valued on the military labor market throughout Europe. It last experienced foreign occupation during the period of French hegemony during the

---

amerikanische Neutralität im Kriege, 1939-1941 (1943).

[4] Admission of a State to the United Nations (Charter, Art. 4), 1948 ICJ Rep. 57, 112 (Advisory Opinion of May 28) (Krylov, J., dissenting).

[5] See Argentine Republic v. Amerada Hess Shipping Corp., 488 U.S. 428 (1989) (no jurisdiction under the Foreign Sovereign Immunities Act to hear a claim Argentina violated neutral rights by attacking neutral on high seas) On the present status of neutrality in general, see Dietrich Schindler, "Transformation of Neutrality since 1945," in Humanitarian Law of Armed C: Challenges Ahead, 367 (Astrid Delimen & Cerard Tanja eds., 1991). For a rare expression of interest in neutrality, see "Neutrality, the Rights of Shipping and the Use of Force in the Persian Gulf War (Parts I & II), 82 in ASIL Proc. 146, 594 (1988).

Napoleanic era, when it was known as the Helvetic Republic. The settlement at the Congress of Vienna produced an international declaration of November 20, 1815 that Switzerland should be "permanently neutral".[6] This status implied obligations for both Switzerland and other states. Switzerland was supposed to refrain from unneutral activities and other states were not to invade the country or interfere with its sovereignty. A rather similar status was imposed on Belgium somewhat later.

Territorial Integrity of a Neutral

The first obligation of a neutral state is to preserve its territorial integrity, that is, not to allow other states to impinge upon its soil or the airspace above it to conduct their warlike activities. Switzerland was not invaded during World War II by either side. However, there were incursions into its airspace by both sides.[7]

For their part, the Germans, during the French campaign in the spring of 1940, sent Luftwaffe units across western Switzerland as a convenient short cut to targets in the area encompassing Dijon and Lyons. Following their neutral duties, Swiss pilots scrambled to meet the challenge. Aerial combat resulted and aircraft were shot down by each side, with the advantage falling to the Swiss. Reportedly, Hitler was extremely angered by this action, all the more because the Swiss air force was flying Messerschmitt fighters sold to it by Germany and because Swiss pilots were hotly pursuing German aircraft into French airspace. He was also annoyed because German troops had found documents in France relating to discussions between the Swiss and French general staffs about the joint operations they would have pursued if the Germans had attacked neutral Switzerland rather than neutral Belgium and Holland. At the same time, the Swiss were interning units

---

[6] Edgar Bonjour, *Geschichte der schweizerischen Neutralität*, ch. 9 (2d ed. 1965). Bonjour discusses the difficult problems of establishing an authentic text of the declaration.

[7] See Kurt Bolliger, "Die Neutralitätswahrung im Luftraum," in *Schwedische und schweizerische Neutralität im Zweiten Weltkrieg*, 236 (Rudolf Bindschedler et al., eds., 1985) (hereinafter *Neutralität*).

of the French army that had retreated to the border rather than surrender to the Wehrmacht – in accordance with principles of neutrality.

During the period between the fall of France and the start of the war against the Soviet Union in the summer of 1941, Switzerland felt, and had good reason to feel, apprehension that it might be next on Hitler's list of targets.[8] Public choice theory would have concluded that Hitler would not attain a net benefit from invading Switzerland, but any theory that depended on Hitler's acting rationally was a dangerous guide to action. Retrospectively, we know what the Swiss did not know then, that the German general staff had been ordered to prepare a contingency plan for "Operation Tannenbaum."[9] Operation Tannenbaum envisaged a swift invasion of Switzerland spearheaded by armor and air units; it recognized the dangers that would be presented if the Swiss adopted the tactic of retreating to the mountains and destroying tunnels and other choke points of communications. In June 1941, however, Hitler's focus shifted east and there was no indication that he again seriously contemplated an attack on Switzerland. During March 1943, a time when Switzerland was becoming more aggressive in its trade negotiations with Germany, the Swiss were somewhat apprehensive about an attack, but there seems to have been no real cause for such concern and the alarm soon subsided.[10]

During the war, Switzerland was never compelled to allow German armed forces transit rights across the country. In this respect it fared better than Sweden.[11] That country's neutrality came into conflict with the German interest in circulating units to and from garrisons in Norway without exposing them to the Royal Navy's attacks on transport ships. While trying to impose limitations on that traffic, Sweden felt compelled

---

[8] See, e.g., Hans Senn, "Schweizerische Dissuasionsstrategie im Zweiten Weltkrieg," in ibid. 197.

[9] For a collection of German war plans envisaging an invasion of Switzerland see Werner Roesch, *Bedrohte Schweiz: Die deutschen Operationsplanungen gegen die Schweiz im Sommer/Herbst 1940 und die Abwehrbereitschaft der Armee im Oktober 1940* (1986).

[10] Werner Rings, *Raubgold aus Deutschland: Die 'Golddrehscheibe' Schweiz im Zweiten Weltkrieg*, 52 (1985).

[11] Ulf Brandell, "Die Transitfrage in der schwedischen Aussenpolitik während des Zweiten Weltkrieges," in *Neutralität*, note 7, 82. For Allied protests, see 11 Whiteman, *Digest* §33, 405-07.

to make concessions to Germany. The same applied to movements by German units across Swedish territory from Norway to Finland. The Germans felt less urgency about traversing Swiss territory since they could reach Italy via the Brenner Pass and other routes even further east. Thus, the only German soldiers who were ever transported across Switzerland were some three thousand troops so severely wounded that Swiss army doctors concluded that they would be unfit for service for a long time.[12]

As for the Allies, they also never invaded Switzerland. But they overflew the country on many occasions.[13] The Swiss were rarely able to intercept these flights, often because they lacked radar and night fighters. Swiss cities were blacked out for a time so as to avoid guiding the raiders. The Allied flights often crossed Switzerland en route from England to targets in northern Italy. In about ten cases, bombs were dropped on Swiss territory. Most notoriously, on April 1, 1944, U.S. fliers attacked Schaffhausen, a Swiss city with the bad luck to be located on the north bank of the Rhine, which, in general, forms the Swiss/ German border as it flows west from Lake Constance. The United States apologized for the action and paid Switzerland compensation for the civilian dead and wounded and for property damage caused by this "violation of neutral rights."[14] In addition, Basel was bombed twice by the Royal Air Force. Once bombs fell ominously close to a ball-bearing factory. Many forced entries into Swiss airspace were by bombers damaged in action over targets in Germany and unable to return home. They usually did not resist the orders of Swiss fighter pilots to land and be interned, though there were occasional misunderstandings due in large part to the fact that the Swiss were still flying Messerschmitts. In one episode, after a raid on Friedrichshafen on the north shore of Lake Constance, sixteen U.S. bombers crash-landed on Swiss soil.[15]

---

[12] Richard Ochsner, "Transit von Trupen, Einzelpersonen, Kriegsmaterial und zivilen Gebrauchsgütern zugunsten der Kriegspartei durch das neutrale Land," in *Neutralität*, supra note 7, 216. Such humanitarian transit is recognized in Article 14 of the Hague Convention on neutrality, see note 17 infra.

[13] Swiss sources meticulously counted 6,501 violations of Swiss airspace. Denis J. Fodor et al., *The Neutrals* (1982).

[14] Whiteman, *Digest*, §9, at 207-09. See "Settlement of Certain War Claims, Oct. 21, 1949. U.S.-Switz.," TIAS, 112, 132 UNTS 163.

[15] Geoffrey Perret, *Winged Victory: The Army Air Forces in World War II* (1993), 292. supra note 12, 219.

In the closing months of the war, the Swiss Government, after considerable soul-searching, decided to permit a substantial deviation from neutral behavior in the matter of troop transports. While the war with Japan was still in progress, some seven hundred thousand British troops without weapons were moved from Italy to Britain for redeployment. It was unlikely that they would be employed in operations against Japan and the Japanese had too many other problems on their hands to file a protest.[16]

In conclusion, one should appreciate that Switzerland's policy of maintaining a substantial portion of its armed forces on a ready status imposed significant costs on the Swiss taxpayer who footed the bill and on the citizen soldiers who for long periods of service were separated from their families and careers. These sacrifices pale into insignificance alongside those made by Allied soldiers who actually fought, but they can be fairly compared with those made by Americans who stood long, boring watches during the Cold War. It is understandable that the self-image of Switzerland in this period still centers on its citizens' belief that a German invasion was prevented by the firm stance of the Swiss armed forces.

Trade by Neutrals

Trade by neutrals with warring parties was permitted under the traditional rules. This extended even to sales of weapons. The only restrictions under the Hague Convention were, first, that any limitations on sales be impartially applied so as not to discriminate between the sides[17] and, second, that the government itself not sell to belligerents.[18]

---

[16] Ochsner, supra note 12, 219.

[17] Hague Convention respecting the Rights and Duties of Neutral Powers and Persons in Case of War on Land. Oct. 18, 1907, Art. 7, 36 Stat. 2310, 1 Bevans, 654: "A neutral Power is not called upon to prevent the export or transport, on behalf of one or other of the belligerents, of arms, munitions of war, or, in general. of anything which can be of use to an army or a fleet." Article 9 reads in part: "Every measure of restriction or prohibition taken by a neutral Power in regard to the matters referred to in Articles 7 and 8 must be impartially applied by it to both belligerents."

[18] This rule is, curiously, to be found in the Hague Convention concerning the Rights and Duties of Neutral Powers in Naval War, Oct. 18, 1907, 36 Stat. 2415, 1 Bevans, 723, to which landlocked Switzerland was a party. Article 6 says: "The

The rule of evenhandedness may in fact produce differential consequences if the geographic/military situation favors one belligerent. The
Swiss decision in the fall of 1939 to sell arms for a time favored France
and Britain, which had put in large orders for Oerlikon antiaircraft
guns.[19] The fall of France gave Germany the advantage in weapons
purchases thereafter, since it was only possible to smuggle small
quantities of specialized components to the West from then until the
summer of 1944. By way of comparison, during World War I Secretary
of State Lansing told the Austro-Hungarian ambassador that the United
States intended to continue its policy of selling arms to all belligerents
and that, if not many sales were made to Germany or Austria, they could
take the matter up with the Royal Navy.[20]

One sees expressions of indignation, in the current writings about
Switzerland during the war, at the fact that the Swiss traded with the
Nazis. This was not only legal, but also inevitable. From the summer of
1940 to the fall of 1944, Switzerland was surrounded on all sides by
Germany and its allies. As a country of some 4.2 million inhabitants, it
was hardly self-sufficient. Before the war, it had produced only about
half of its food supply; for much of the war period, its citizens lived on
short rations comparable to those prevailing in the belligerent states.[21]
It also needed coal, petroleum products and raw materials to keep its
factories going and to provide employment. There are statements from
the Nazi camp that Switzerland was indispensable to the German
economic war effort, in particular financial assistance.[22]

Two things may be noted about that commerce: First, the trade was,
after all, bilateral. While Switzerland was supplying Germany with
weapons, electricity, machinery, Germany was constantly shipping
goods to Switzerland that would have been useful to its war effort if

---

supply, in any manner, directly or indirectly, by a neutral Power to a belligerent
Power, of warships, ammunition, or war material of any kind whatever, is
forbidden."

[19]Klaus Urner, "Neutralität und Wirtschaftskrieg: Zur schweizerischen Aussenhandelspolitik," in *Neutralität*, supra note 7, 256, 266-73.

[20] 7 Hackworth, Digest §684, 618-20.

[21] Jerrold M. Packard, *Neither Friend nor Foe: The European Neutrals in
World War II* (1992), 249-52.

[22] Walter Funk, Reich Minister of Economics, is cited to that effect. Rings,
supra note 10, 7.

retained in Germany. A fraction of German exports paid for invisible items on the Swiss side, such as interest on loans and insurance premiums, of no use to the war effort. It is therefore misleading to think of Swiss exports as simply a net gain to the Nazi war effort. Second, the Allies were fully informed about Swiss trade with the Germans, just as the Germans were kept appraised of Swiss trade with the Allies. Because there was a series of agreements, renewed about twice a year, between the Swiss and Germans and the Swiss and the Allies,[23] each could be said to have consented to the trade with the adversary. That consent was necessary because the Germans could bar all traffic across their territory in a form of counter-blockade. The Allies, while the territory they controlled was not contiguous to Switzerland, could prevent it from trading with neutrals, as well as themselves, through the British "navicert" system and the blacklisting of Swiss firms doing business with Germany without tacit leave.

Predictably, the terms of the trade agreements shifted with the tides of war. Except for fanatic Nazis, Europeans recognized in the summer of 1943 that with the great Nazi defeat at Kursk and the Allied landing in Sicily, which precipitated the fall of the Fascist Government, Hitler's days were numbered. Therefore, the renewals of the trade agreement with Germany were on different terms. For one thing, the Germans were experiencing increasing difficulties in living up to their commitments to furnish coal, owing to the disruptions in the rail system, shortages of labor and heavy bombing of the Ruhr mining district. Allied pressures to disengage from Germany increased. At the same time, Swiss exports of armaments and components for arms for the third quarter of 1944 amounted to only 10 percent of the quantity shipped in 1942. Arms exports stopped completely in September 1944 as Western troops reached the border.[24]

Two aspects of Swiss trade practice seem vulnerable to criticism as departures from the legal rules on neutrality. First, the Swiss Government in effect advanced funds to Germany so that it could import Swiss goods; the matter became interwoven with the issues regarding the gold that flowed into Switzerland from Germany (discussed below). Second,

---

[23] For a description of these by a negotiator see Heinrich Homberger, *Schweizerische Handelspolitik im Zweiten Weltkrieg* (1970).

[24] Ibid., 109-12.

in 1941 under German pressure, Switzerland forbade the export of goods through the mails; this ban had the effect of virtually terminating the practice of sending small, but valuable, arms components to the Allies. At that time, Germany had not fully taken the matter into its own hands by controlling traffic through unoccupied France.[25]

Neutrals as Intermediaries

One of the classic activities of a neutral is the furnishing of good offices to the warring parties. Sometimes this activity has been spectacularly successful, as when Russia and Japan ended their war on President Theodore Roosevelt's yacht in the harbor of Portsmouth, New Hampshire. Antagonism between the sides in World War II reached such a level of intensity that Switzerland could not effectively perform this function. There was no room for negotiation in the face of the demand for unconditional surrender. Negotiations did take place in Switzerland for the separate surrender of the German armed forces in Italy. Acute concerns of the negotiators on both sides that Stalin and Hitler might hear about this settlement delayed it to the point that the separate surrender only narrowly preceded the final surrender celebrated as V-E Day.[26] The Swiss communications system proved technically useful in passing the messages back and forth between Japan and the Allies that led to the ceremonies of surrender celebrated as V-J Day.[27]

One chapter of Swiss intermediation deserves special mention. Switzerland was designated by both Germany and the Western Allies as the protecting power under the Geneva Convention of 1929 with respect to prisoners of war.[28] That conditions for British and American prisoners of war never descended to the levels that prevailed in other camps run by the German Government is in no small measure due to the presence of Swiss inspectors. The contrast is particularly sharp when one looks

---

[25] Urner, supra note 19, 281.

[26] Richard Lamb, *War in Italy: A Brutal Story, 1943-45* (1993), 284-289.

[27] Konrad Stamm, "Die Vertretung fremder Interessen durch die Schweiz im Zweiten Weltkrieg," in *Neutralität*, supra note 7, 307, 312-14.

[28] Convention Relative to the Treatment of Prisoners of War, July 27, 1929, Art. 86, 47 Stat. 2021, 2 Bevans, 932.

at the appalling mortality rates in camps where captives from the Red Army were confined without coverage under the Convention.[29] Although Japan was a signatory to the 1929 Convention, its authorities refused to take it seriously and Swiss emissaries accomplished little, one of them even being executed by the Japanese in the process.[30] Delegates from the International Committee of the Red Cross (ICRC) accepted the growing risks connected with travel through wartime Germany in order to ensure observance of the Convention. Their presence, inter alia, reminded German camp administrators that delinquencies on their part would be communicated to the Western powers, which were increasingly in a position to retaliate as their inventory of German POWs grew. In one episode the Swiss were able to persuade the British and the Germans to cease putting their prisoners in handcuffs, a practice that had developed into a cycle of retaliation.[31] At the same time, the Red Cross was able to bring to the camps under its supervision both mail from home and packages of food and other necessities and amenities of life that the Germans were unwilling or unable to provide.

The ICRC has come under criticism of late from Swiss sources on the grounds that it drew its mandate too narrowly and, in the interest of preserving the smooth functioning of its prisoner-of-war operations, suppressed the information it possessed about the fate of civilian inmates of the death camps. Resolution of that question implicates such issues as whether a protest to Germany about the Final Solution would have mitigated the horrors of the Holocaust or seriously harmed the POW work by terminating German cooperation.[32] Similar questions are raised about the reactions of the Western Allies and the papacy to learning – at about the same time – the essential facts about the Holocaust. Toward the end of the war, the ICRC did begin to pay more attention to civilian detainees and other nonmilitary captives of the Nazis. The ICRC and other Swiss functionaries helped make arrangements with Nazi leaders that brought 1,368 Jews from Bergen-Belsen to

---

[29] Christian Streit, *Keine Kameraden: Die Wehrmacht und die sowjetischen Kriegsgefangenen, 1941-1945* (1978), 10.

[30] Stamm, supra note 27, 314-15.

[31] Erwin Bucher, *Zwischen Bundesrat und General* (1993), 588.

[32] Jean-Claude Favez, *Une mission impossible? Le CICR, les déportations et les camps de concentration nazis* (1988), 367-75.

Switzerland and another 1,200 from Theresienstadt, although other negotiations broke down.[33] Swiss agents in Hungary distributed documents to Jews that placed them under Swiss protection and spared them from the worst. This activity closely paralleled the better-known work of the Swedish delegate Raoul Wallenberg, who disappeared into Russian hands. As soon as the fighting stopped, the Swiss Red Cross was well positioned to bring relief supplies to the concentration camps swiftly and efficiently.

Refugee Policy

The real blot on Switzerland's honor lies in its treatment of some refugees from the Nazi horrors. Neutrals have a right and at least a moral obligation to provide shelter for those attempting to flee war, persecution and their attendant cruelties. However, at that time, each country, including the United States, regarded how many refugees of what types it would admit to be a matter within its domestic jurisdiction. Objectionable Swiss practices began with persuading the Germans to adopt the practice of stamping the passports of German Jews with a "J."[34] [This claim recently has been disproved-Ed.]. This episode is difficult to understand, partly because the German Government had already issued rules that would shortly force upon its Jewish population the adoption of Sara or Israel as first names. The fact that the "J" stamp was instituted at the behest of the Swiss Government was carefully concealed from the public.

Most dreadful is the turning away of some twenty thousand Jews who were attempting to escape from Nazism in 1942 after the nature of the threat to them from the Holocaust had become apparent, at least to policy-making members of the Swiss Government. The latter instituted a policy of rejecting claims for refugee status based on race, as differentiated from politics. The persons most affected were refugees from France, since reaching the Swiss border through Germany was already impossible. There was considerable protest within Switzerland as the reality became known and eventually the policy was relaxed, but much

---

[33] Jacques Picard, *Die Schweiz und die Juden 1933-1945* (1994), 455-61.

[34] Ibid., 157-62. [This claim has recently been proven as being false. Ed.]

too late to avoid the destruction of these unfortunate would-be émigrés. Belatedly, the Swiss President apologized for this action during the proceedings commemorating the fiftieth anniversary of the end of World War II. The enormity of this cruel action quite overshadows the fact that it did not violate international law as it was understood in 1942. The matter became subject to international law only with the adoption of the Protocol Relating to the Status of Refugees.[35] The Swiss delegation at the drafting conference in Geneva argued vigorously for the proposition that a state should retain the right to turn back people who had not yet been admitted to its territory. It said: "According to that interpretation, States were not compelled to allow large groups of persons claiming refugee status to cross its [sic] frontiers." It thus justified the past behavior of Switzerland during World War II and reserved its right to act in the same way in the future. One is disturbed to find that the United States Supreme Court quoted extensively from that Swiss argumentation when it upheld the administration's practice of intercepting refugees on the way from Haiti to the United States.[36]

The Swiss rejection of these terribly endangered persons took place in the context of the country's acceptance of a very substantial number – apparently nearly three hundred thousand – of refugees of various categories from 1933 onward.[37] That figure includes escaped prisoners of war, soldiers seeking internment, Italians and French fleeing the oncoming fighting, and others. In relation to a population of 4.2 million, the figure compares favorably with the number admitted during that time by the United States and Great Britain. It also compares favorably with reactions by the United States with regard to Haiti, and by European countries, including Germany, with respect to the former Yugoslavia. The Swiss argument that the "boat is full" was not without some measure of validity. Among the persons who did succeed in attaining asylum in Switzerland were those who entered unlawfully with the assistance of officials and other Swiss sympathizers, Jewish and gentile. It is a symptom of Swiss hyper-legalism that the most famous

---

[35] Jan. 31, 1967, 19 UST 6223, 606 UNTS 267.

[36] Sale vs. Haitian Centers Council, Inc., 509 U.S. (1993), 155, 184-187.

[37] Raul Hilberg, *Perpetrators, Victims, Bystanders: The Jewish Catastrophe 1933-1945* (1992), 258.

official to assist Jewish refugees by irregular means, Paul Grüninger, was not "rehabilitated" until 1993.[38]

Financial Matters

The original focus of the revived interest in Swiss behavior in the 1940s was the issue of numbered bank accounts maintained in Swiss institutions by persons who had perished in the Holocaust. This Editorial Comment will not consider that subject since it is not a matter of public international law but of actions by private institutions and, incidentally, because the facts are at this point so unclear that it is hard to comment meaningfully on the complex of issues. However, that complex of issues is related to the financial activities of the Swiss Government, in particular to claims that have been or might be raised by other governments.

During the war, the Swiss Government, the Swiss national bank and private institutions entered into dealings with the German Government and German individuals. There was nothing inconsistent with the status of neutrality in those activities per se. However, the origins of the German assets transferred to Switzerland were in some cases of such a shadowy character as to raise questions. For one thing, there were movements to Switzerland of the monetary gold reserves of the governments and central banks of states that had come under Nazi control in 1940. This practice has evoked many expressions of shock in recent discussions of "looted gold" and Switzerland's behavior. Its illegality under the rules then in place, however, is not that clear. Those rules were stated in the Regulations annexed to the 1907 Hague Convention respecting the Laws and Customs of War on Land.[39] Switzerland could rely on Article 53, which says that "[a]n army of occupation can only take possession of cash, funds, and realizable securities which are strictly the property of the State." To that extent, the Convention carried forward the old "to the victor belong the spoils" tradition. Article 46 of the Regulations provides that "[p]rivate property cannot be confiscated." There is room for argument as to whether the

---

[38] Picard, supra note 33, 301-302.
[39] Oct. 18, 1907, 36 Stat. 2277, 1 Bevans 631.

holdings of central banks sometimes incorporated under commercial laws, were "strictly the property of the State" or were private.

There is also a possible argument that such seizures violated Article 55, which limits occupying states in their utilization of the wealth of defeated countries to that of a usufructuary, that is, a life tenant. Taking the wealth of an occupied country in such a way as to deprive it permanently of these resources might violate that provision. Swiss state responsibility would be derivative of the German. Although the law of involvement in international wrongs by states that in municipal legal systems might be categorized as co-conspirators, joint tortfeasors, aiders and abetttors, or receivers of stolen property was not well developed in the 1940s (and is not far advanced today), it could be argued that Switzerland did incur such responsibility. That reasoning would require dealing with such possible defenses by Switzerland as that it had acted in good faith, ignorant of the precise origins of the gold, that it had passed the gold on to other states, and that it was entitled to a setoff for funds advanced to Germany. Swiss bankers in 1944 obtained an opinion about the legal questions from an eminent Swiss international lawyer, Dietrich Schindler, and in 1946, in preparation for negotiations with the Allies, obtained another opinion from the equally distinguished Georges Sauser-Hall.[40] Different questions would arise to the extent that it was shown that the gold had been private both under the Hague Convention and under general human rights law.

As a matter of strict international law, the questions were laid to rest by the so-called Washington Accord of 1946 in which a lump sum settlement was agreed upon by the parties involved.[41] The negotiations were arduous. Stubbornly, the Swiss Government clung to the position that it was "unable to recognize the legal basis for these claims" but asserted that it "desired to contribute its share to the pacification and reconstruction of Europe." It argued that Allied economic warfare measures against Switzerland, such as the blacklisting of Swiss firms and the freezing of Swiss assets, had been of doubtful legality during the war, and in peacetime were clear violations of its rights. The agreement called for a settlement of gold claims for 250 million Swiss francs. It

---

[40] Rings, supra note 10, 79, 110-13.
[41] Liquidation of German Property in Switzerland, May 25, 1946, 13 UST 1118.

also required Switzerland to round up assets in Switzerland held by Germans resident in Germany and turn part of them over to the Allied occupation authorities in Germany, who assumed responsibility for compensating the German owners. That obligation was assumed by the Federal Republic and compensation was eventually paid by it.[42] We have recently learned that there was a postwar agreement between Switzerland and Poland transferring Polish assets in Switzerland to the Swiss Government, which used them to compensate Swiss citizens whose assets in Poland had been expropriated. Poland assumed responsibility for reimbursing its nationals.[43] Unlike the Washington Accord, this agreement was secret and acknowledgment of its existence had to be wrung out of the Bern Government inch by inch.

Is there any reason to suppose that the Washington Accord might be regarded as invalid under international law? The Vienna Convention on the Law of Treaties sets up several reasons for invalidating treaties, including counterparts to the standard municipal law grounds for setting aside contracts.[44] These include coercion, fraud and mistake. It seems a bit implausible to think that Switzerland could exert coercion on states whose armed forces had just crushed the Third Reich. Additionally, large amounts of Swiss funds in the United States were frozen under the Trading with the Enemy Act and only released after the Washington Accord. There is little authority on "fraud" or "mistake" under international law.

The accounts standing between Switzerland and Germany and the occupied states were complex and subject to argument. The Allied Governments were represented by a distinguished delegation – the United States mission chief was the noted tax lawyer Randolph Paul – and had information both from the states whose gold was taken and from captured German documents and witnesses. Everybody in 1946

---

[42]There was a later agreement of Aug. 28, 1952, Liquidation of German Property in Switzerland, 13 UST 1131, which involved transfers among Germany, Switzerland and the Allied powers to settle the German property claims. The Swiss Government asserted that there were no assets of "heirless Nazi victims" but stated that it would give sympathetic consideration to their dedication to a charitable cause if any were found thereafter. See the letter related to the agreement, Aug. 28, 1952, ibid., 1143.

[43] *Frankfurter Allgemeine Zeitung*, March 14, 1997, 58-59.

[44] *Opened for signature* May 23, 1969, 1155 UNTS 331.

was anxious to get on with the business of rebuilding Europe and to set the past aside. There was general gratitude toward Switzerland for the past work of the ICRC and other Swiss agencies and an expectation that Swiss relief work would continue into the postwar reconstruction period. There was perhaps some embarrassment over the as yet unsettled claims from bomb damage to Switzerland. And there was anxiety about communism. The negotiators accepted the accord, lest "an agreement with ţhe Swiss, which would secure whole-hearted support by the Swiss of the Allied economic security objective, should be jeopardized for the sake of a few more dollars."[45] Shortly before that point, Winston Churchill had written Anthony Eden words the Swiss are prone to quote:

> Of all the neutrals Switzerland has the greatest right to distinction. She has been the sole international force linking the hideously sundered nations and ourselves. What does it matter whether she has been able to give us the commercial advantages we desire or has given too many to the Germans, to keep herself alive? She has been a democratic state, standing for freedom in self-defence among her mountains, and in thought, in spite of race, largely on our side.[46]

For the states involved to take a crude stab at a total figure seems an entirely natural thing to have done. It has been standard practice to settle international claims by quite gross lump sum settlements. Any claim for the invalidity of the Washington Accord seems farfetched. As this Comment went to press, the U.S. Government issued a report sharply critical of the accord, but no move to set it aside seems to be in prospect.[47]

Conclusion

On the whole, the behavior of the Swiss Government during World War II was in compliance with the rules of international law, including

---

[45] *Foreign Relations of the United States* (1946), 216.

[46] Winston Churchill, *The Second World War.* Vol. 6: *Triumph and Tragedy* (London: Cassell, 1954), 616; quoted in Homberger, supra note 23, 131, and Bucher, supra note 31, 589. The context of the quotation was advice to Anthony Eden about the position the allies should take regarding Switzerland vis-à-vis Stalin.

[47] *New York Times*, May 8, 1997, A1.

the rules of neutrality, as they were then understood. There were lapses in connection with trade and transit, though some of them leaned in favor of the Allies. With respect to the gold transactions, it does appear that there were violations of international law, but that fifty years ago a reasonable and binding settlement of those claims was achieved. A case can be made for the proposition that the trespasses on Switzerland's rights as a neutral that were committed by the warring parties were substantially more serious than the Swiss lapses. When one passes from legal to moral questions, the issues become much more subjective and this Comment cannot deal confidently with them. It is, however, worthwhile to think about Winston Churchill's contemporaneous judgment, that of a statesman being one who knew how difficult it was to navigate the ship of state in such turbulent waters.

EPILOGUE: SUMMARY VIEW OF
SWITZERLAND IN WORLD WAR II

Sigmund Widmer

Between Two Wars

Switzerland's situation during the First World War – that of a small state caught between two large warring coalitions – corresponded exactly to the circumstances that over the centuries had pushed the country to adopt a policy of neutrality. At the end of a conflict from which she had been spared, Switzerland was in a position to publicly take some constructive initiatives on an international level. Such was the project for a new organization for world peace: the League of Nations. Under the presidency of Federal Councilor Calonder, a task force drew up the statutes of a pacific international organization based on the project of Max Huber (an eminent Swiss lawyer and future president of the International Committee of the Red Cross, a purely Swiss institution). This, notably, included the participation of neutral states. Geneva could already pride itself on its traditional links to the Red Cross and was allocated the headquarters of the League of Nations.[1] Switzerland's open attitude also led to the choice of this country as the venue for important international conferences such as that of Locarno in 1925.

Nevertheless, by 1938, the growing tension on the world's political scene was to lead Switzerland back to "full" neutrality, which most of its citizens perceived as armed neutrality.[2] Accordingly, this little

---

[1] Footnotes by Georges-André Cuendet.

[2] The return to "full" neutrality (after "differential" neutrality in the preceding years) followed a decision taken by the League of Nations to enforce economic sanctions against Italy following its invasion of Ethiopia in 1936. By pleading its neutrality and proximity to Italy, Switzerland – at the instigation of the Federal Councilor Giuseppe Motta – distanced herself from these sanctions; a move which was qualified by the *Manchester Guardian* as "particularly disgraceful" and was severely judged within Switzerland.

country came to play a much greater role in the strategic calculations of the major powers in comparison with nations like Belgium and Holland.

In the 1930s, along with most other countries across the globe, Switzerland was severely hit by the economic crisis. The decision taken on September 26, 1936 to devalue the franc by 30% certainly helped to overcome this problem. Of greater importance, however, was the establishment of a calm social climate because of peaceful labor relations.[3] This internal peace was an essential prerequisite which helped in facing up to the much more serious challenges posed by the Second World War.

The 1939 National Exhibition

With an unofficial rhythm of every 25 years, it was fortuitous that a national exhibition was scheduled to take place in Zürich during the summer of 1939.[4] Preparations for it had already started at the beginning of the 1930s, which shows the event was initially motivated to address the economic crisis. The hazards of world politics meant that the "Landi" (a Swiss-German abbreviation for the exhibition) went far beyond this economic aspect to become a demonstration of national unity. Differences between political parties vanished in the face of external threats, in particular those of National Socialism in Germany and Fascism in Italy. A sentiment of national unity took precedence over political differences as well as cultural and linguistic ones.

Mobilization – 1939

Such concord in national opinion was essential for the smooth implementation of general mobilization when the Second World War

---

[3] The agreement for "peaceful labor relations" in the metal-working industry was signed on July 19, 1937. It removed the possibility of resorting to strikes and lock-outs and served as a model for similar agreements in other sectors.

[4] Opened on May 6, 1939 on a site covering both banks of the Lake of Zürich at the entrance to the city, the national exhibition received 10 million visitors (almost as many as the 11.5 million who attended the Expo 64 in Lausanne). It triggered the following comment from the *Deutsche Allgemeine Zeitung*: "This visit leaves one with the distinct feeling that the (Swiss) population wants to defend itself and claim its right to exist".

broke out. The fast and almost unanimous choice of General Guisan illustrated this. It went without saying that the commander-in-chief of the army had to be a French-Swiss, that is, from the linguistic and cultural minority.[5] The mobilization did however bring to light notorious shortcomings. There were no plans for troop deployment and, above all, weaponry was seriously lacking in some areas[6], the reasons for which were clear: an incorrect but widespread belief at the beginning of the 1920s that after the catastrophe of the First World War, never again would there be a major conflict. This prompted various factions – in particular the Social Democratic Party – to refuse budget allocations for armament and even to oppose military service. Once Hitler had taken power in 1933 there was a definite effort to make up for lost time but, in 1936, the Socialist party once again refused to agree to a "defense loan" aimed at accelerating the financing of necessary weapons.[7]

The general and his senior officers were aware that their available forces were insufficient to defend Switzerland along her borders. Guisan therefore decided upon what was known as the "Limmat Defense Line". It ran from Sargans, near the Upper Rhine, as far as the Jura (where it linked up with the French Maginot Line) passing along the banks of the lakes of Walenstadt and Zürich, then following the course of the river Limmat. This strategy took into account the secret agreement that Guisan had negotiated with France in the event of a German offensive in Switzerland. Conversely, it had already been decided in September 1939 that an important part of the country, including the towns of Basel,

---

[5] General Henri Guisan (1874-1960) was elected on August 30, 1939 by the Federal Assembly two days before hostilities started. He obtained 204 votes out of 225 votes cast.

[6] At the outbreak of the war Switzerland had only a pitiful airforce comprising 18 fighter planes fit for combat, 36 outdated aircraft, and 80 observation planes (by comparison, Germany engaged 3,000 aircraft in the Polish campaign and in two days wiped out the Polish airforce which had 800 planes).

[7] It should be noted, however, that the 1937 Social Democrat Congress overwhelmingly approved national military defense. It should be mentioned here that the Confederation twice levied a special wealth tax – once in 1940 and again in 1942 – called the "sacrificial tax" to increase the state's other resources. From 1941 among these resources was the "national defense tax" (IDN) which survives today under the name of the "direct federal tax" (IFD).

Schaffhausen, Winterthur, and St. Gallen would be left with little defense.

Mobilization was to turn everyday life in Switzerland upside-down. Workmen of every kind were removed from their workplace, and women frequently replaced them. For many self-employed people, military service presented a serious risk to the survival of their businesses. As Switzerland felt directly threatened by Germany and expected an imminent attack, leave was granted very sparingly, in any event at least until the end of the winter of 1939/40.[8]

Supplies

Long before the Second World War broke out, it was a recognized fact in Switzerland that being a densely populated country with few natural resources, it could not be self-sufficient. The government had made sure – through efficient rationing – that available foodstuffs and vital raw materials were distributed fairly. The urban population was consequently forced into a simple lifestyle, not to say a rigorous one which Swiss people today would have difficulty imagining. At the same time, an extended cultivation program was put into effect under the name of the "Wahlen Plan" (named after its initiator who was later to become a Federal Councilor). It is clear that measures such as the intensive use of agricultural lands, the appropriation of gardens and public parks for the cultivation of vegetables and potatoes, the clearance of forests on the plains did help to reduce Switzerland's dependence on imported foodstuffs, but these measures were not enough to assure the country's self-sufficiency.[9] This was particularly so in the case of the vital coal supplies from Germany, without which the economy would have been quickly paralyzed for lack of sufficient alternative fuel sources. This fundamental element must be taken into account when evaluating Switzerland's actions during the Second World War.

---

[8] Mobilization affected some 440,000 men out of a total population of just over 4 million people.

[9] In accordance with the Wahlen Plan, the area under cultivation increased from 450,000 to 870,000 acres (180,000 to 350,000 hectares), which made it possible to cover more than 50% of the country's dietary needs.

May 1940

As in the case of the Allied forces, the "Phony War" had an effect on the morale of the Swiss troops. They started to get bored. Many commanding officers fought this state of mind by quick changes in stationing and frequent alarm exercises with night-time maneuvers. The Winter War in Finland helped to strengthen the troops' morale: a small country demonstrated how, helped by the natural environment, it was possible to resist a major power siding with Nazi Germany. Confidence in Switzerland's ability to resist was reinforced considerably.

The daily monotony was interrupted early in May by rumors concerning the movement of German units on the north bank of the Rhine. It was, therefore, almost with relief that the troops received the news of the attack on Belgium and the Netherlands on May 10, 1940. However, the civilian population reacted very differently. The people had not been aware of the movement of German troops on the north bank of the Rhine, intended to divert attention, and were taken by surprise by the German offensive to such a point that there were moments of panic, especially along the borders. Cities like Zürich witnessed a real exodus of civilians towards central Switzerland. There was a dangerous social component in these movements as those fleeing were mainly from the wealthier social classes.

Summer 1940

The progress of the fighting in Western Europe turned out to be crucial to the subsequent course of events. With its "sickle swing" Germany had separated the French and English troops and drawn the forces of the former away from their defense lines. Despite Germany's spectacular successes and the British evacuation at Dunkirk, nobody in Switzerland had anticipated the speed of the German advance. There was far more reference to the 1914 "miracle of the Marne", in the hope that events would follow the same course. The rapid collapse of France, called *La Grande Nation*, the "Great Nation", was consequently viewed with that much more anxiety by the Swiss because they saw the entry of Hitler's divisions into Paris as a catastrophe touching them directly. These feelings – that today's generations have difficulty in imagining –

did not just prevail in the French part of Switzerland; more particularly, they served to put into perspective the famous speech delivered by Marcel Pilet-Golaz, the President of the Swiss Confederation, on June 25, 1940, the first day of the French armistice.[10]

It is also important at this point to recall the attitude of the United States. The country deliberately stood back from the events in Europe, declaring itself (like Switzerland) neutral but not averse to obtaining some financial gains from the events. It was not until the attack on Pearl Harbor on December 7, 1941 followed immediately by Germany's arrogant declaration of war on the United States that America actively sided with the other democracies.

Retreat into the Redoubt

It is against this background that General Guisan's retreat into the "Redoubt" must be understood.[11] As pointed out above, from the very beginning Switzerland had decided not to defend her borders. During the summer of 1940 what she did was to take another step – certainly an important one – in the same direction. The idea of the "Redoubt" grew from the desire to put up as much dogged resistance as possible to an enemy overwhelmingly superior in numbers, using all means available, and making full use of the terrain. Today it is easy to forget that there was no question of abandoning the Swiss lowlands without a fight. The

---

[10] In this broadcast speech, Pilet-Golaz appealed for an "internal revival" and asked the population to have "full confidence" in the Federal Council. Public opinion was shocked by this speech because in it the author welcomed "with great relief" peace imposed on a defeated France and made allusions to "a new European balance away from outdated concepts." However clumsy and questionable these comments might have been, it would be wrong to deduce from them that the Federal Council recommended that Switzerland "align" with the Hitlerite order. The greatest weakness in Pilet-Golaz's speech was that it did not answer justified questions, in particular as to whether the government wanted to resist.

[11] The idea of the redoubt was to revive an old strategic idea whereby the main forces would be concentrated in the central Alpine massif behind the bastions composed of the fortifications of Sargans, the Gotthard and Saint Maurice, effectively blocking all passages through the Alps. Inaccessible to armoured vehicles and scarcely favorable for air warfare, such a redoubt could only have been conquered by a foreign army at heavy costs.

idea was to put up a tenacious resistance to delay the invaders, using the newly built fortifications as bases. It was this same idea that inspired the planned destruction of all usable industrial installations and electricity and water grids. Every bridge had been mined. When some historians today view the "Redoubt" concept as a gesture of "submission" to Hitler, they are displaying their total ignorance of the then prevailing conditions.

Frontists and Communists

As it has become fashionable in some circles to pretend that Switzerland was favorable to Nazism during the war, it is necessary to recall the facts. In 1933, under the influence of Hitler's rise to power in Germany and his initial successes, notably in the fight against unemployment, a "National Front" was formed in Switzerland. Nevertheless, it never succeeded in obtaining more than a single seat in the federal parliament (held by the Zürich representative R. Tobler in 1935), who lost it again in 1939. With the opening of hostilities and Switzerland's given political leanings since 1939, the National Front split into various groups that were finally banned by the Federal Council.

The Communist Party was subject to similar bans at almost the same time. This party had experienced its apogee after the First World War when Lenin triumphed in Russia and it had boomed again in the 1930s with the economic crisis. However, the pact made between Hitler and Stalin in 1939 dealt it a blow from which it did not recover. In view of the ban imposed on the Communist Party in Switzerland, another group pledging alliance to the Soviet Union replaced it towards the end of the war under the name of "the workers' party". In other words, the two totalitarian regimes never managed to get a foothold in Switzerland, mainly because labor relations upheld the Swiss democratic system and because the "Labor Peace Treaty", in force since 1937, encouraged cooperation between the workers' unions and the employers' organizations.

Censorship

If there is one thing for which Switzerland should be criticized during the Second World War, it is probably for the restrictions imposed on the rights of direct democratic and democratic institutions. At the beginning of the war, the Federal Assembly granted the Federal Council "full powers". So that crisis situations could be dealt with rapidly, Parliament relinquished a large part of its authority which was transferred to a "full powers commission". This state of affairs remained until 1949, when the full powers system was abolished and the constitutional order completely reestablished.

The infringement of civil liberties resulted at that time in extensive censorship of the media, essentially the printed press. Understandably, the Federal Council feared that the Swiss newspapers' criticism of Nazism would arouse the anger of Hitler and his henchmen, but the monitoring went too far. Many newspapers such as the *Nebelspalter*, the *Nation*, the *Neue Zürcher Zeitung* (NZZ) and the *Basler Nachrichten* did manage to circumvent the censorship to some extent. With hindsight, this restriction of freedom of opinion is far from glorious, even when taking into account that it was not motivated by political beliefs but rather a desire to avoid provoking an unpredictable tyrant.

Refugees

There is no doubt that looking back, in the climate of security we enjoy today, we would all have been happy to have taken in more refugees, particularly Jewish ones. An objective assessment of the facts does, however, require an analysis of the reasons for adopting a refugee policy which is seen today as restrictive.[12]

As mentioned above, Switzerland was not in a position to guarantee the subsistence of its inhabitants with its own resources. Consequently, it was the Federal Council's mission to make sure the Swiss people did not suffer from famine. This is where the "arable land battle" (*Anbauschlacht* in German) and rationing played their part, but there was also restrictive immigration processing.

Today there is a tendency to criticize the authorities of the time for not having been able to predict, in 1943, the outcome of the war. To

---

[12] The number of refugees admitted each year fluctuated between a minimum of some 10,000 in 1942, the year in which the policy was the most restrictive, and rose to 75,000 at the end of 1943 and to just over 100,000 at the end of the war. In total some 300,000 refugees were sheltered during the war.

claim that Switzerland had nothing more to fear from that moment on does however constitute a typical judgment on the basis of hindsight. The reality was quite different, as may be seen in the following examples. In May 1944, Hitler decided to occupy Hungary to reinforce his Eastern front. Based on the same argument, he could have subsequently "integrated" Switzerland as well. After announcing them in a blaze of publicity, Hitler launched the first V2 missiles in September 1944. England had no means to parry these weapons of terror and the evacuation of London was considered once again.[13] Supposing the German specialists had had more time to carry out their work (in particular on the atomic weapon), the outcome of the war could have been very different. These kinds of examples are numerous.[14] In short, for Switzerland the situation remained menacing at that time until the end of 1944 and, consequently, the idea of throwing open the borders was totally unrealistic.

Nor should it be forgotten that it was not necessarily in the interest of the Jewish community living in Switzerland to see an even greater number of their co-religionists arriving in the country. It could have provided Hitler with a pretext for meddling in Switzerland's domestic affairs. This makes it easy to understand why the Jewish organizations in Switzerland remained relatively discreet concerning the federal authorities' immigration policy.[15]

Today's critics keep quiet about the fact that in 1918, at the end of the First World War, Switzerland had been severely reprimanded by the western democracies for having pursued a generous refugee policy.

---

[13] The V2 missiles carried one ton of explosives and flew at an altitude of 47 miles (75km) and a speed of 3,750 mph (6,000 kmph). The Germans launched 1,300, of which 500 fell on London, killing several thousand people.

[14] The last German offensive on the Western front in the Ardennes, began on 16th December 1944 involving 250,000 men – with 970 tanks and 1,500 aircraft – who briefly succeeded in breaking through the American lines. Despite ceaseless air raids, Germany also had managed to increase its armament production to record levels until the autumn of 1944; for example, 40,953 machines left the aeronautical factories during 1944. In 1945 she still put 82 divisions, albeit weakened, against the Allied army on the Rhine Front.

[15] The number of Jews who found refuge in Switzerland is estimated to be around 29,000. In addition to these refugees, some 20,000 Jews were already living in the country, a little over one half of whom held Swiss nationality.

Switzerland was accused at the time of having become a revolutionary center, with the example of Lenin to support this claim.[16] The greatest revolutionary of the century had actually lived undisturbed in Switzerland for several years. It was from Zürich that, in 1917, he was repatriated in the famous "sealed railway carriage" to Russia where he sparked off a revolution which was to shake the whole world. The traumatic effect of this on the Swiss authorities was long lasting, and thereafter they were careful to avoid criticism for a lax asylum policy.

An objective appreciation of facts shows that Switzerland's refugee policy during the Second World War was fundamentally no different from that of the United States, the country which in the meantime has become its main accuser. Taking into account its size and population, Switzerland's refugee policy was markedly more open than America's.[17]

It is just as contrary to reality to claim that Switzerland as a whole knew about the atrocities being committed in the Nazi concentration camps. Isolated individuals may have known, but it was not until spring 1945 that the Swiss people discovered with horror the photographic evidence of the abominations in the death camps.[18]

Finally, we must recall relations which touch on domestic policy between the question of refugees and the current political environment in Switzerland. During the Second World War the Federal State was a "bourgeois" one, unlike Sweden for example. Among the comparable European countries, Switzerland is the only one to have never been ruled by a left-wing majority. Consequently, it becomes easier to

---

[16] During the First World War, 1,500 Russians and nearly 20,000 deserters and draft dodgers found refuge in Switzerland. Some foreign commentators had begun to spread the idea that Switzerland had become a dangerous center of contagion for the whole of Europe. As absurd as it may seem, this opinion was taken so seriously in the European chanceries and in Washington that they toyed with the idea of the Entente countries taking police action against Switzerland with military means. (Werner Rings, *La Suisse et la Guerre*. Zürich: Ex Libris, 1975, p. 117).

[17] During the war the United States took in about 170,000 Jewish refugees, representing 0.1 % of the population at that time (against 0.7% for Switzerland).

[18] In reality Switzerland was one of the first countries, together with the United States, where, from the summer of 1944, the press started publishing information about the extermination camps, but the extent of the genocide did not come to light until the camps were liberated: Auschwitz on January 27, 1945 ("Auschwitz", published by the Auschwitz-Birkenau Museum, 1994).

understand that some circles are now trying to put this bourgeois Switzerland in the dock.

Gold Policy

That Hitler's Germany robbed Belgium, among others, of her gold reserves was nothing unusual for a victorious country. When the French invaded Switzerland in 1798, one of the reasons for the expedition was to help themselves to the well-filled coffers of the thrifty and puritanical city states of Bern and Zürich. The French troops brought their booty back to Paris without anyone ever speaking of restitution. In the light of the political considerations mentioned above, the gold stolen by the Germans plays an important part. Some hope to incriminate bourgeois Switzerland, above all the National Bank. The unilateral description of the question in the Bergier Commission's intermediate report has already given rise to criticism.

Let's not overdo it! Of course, today, we would all be delighted if the National Bank had never bought an ounce of gold from Nazi Germany. We must not forget, however, that between 1940 and the beginning of 1945 Switzerland's situation in regard to Germany was very precarious. It was not easy for her to estimate the risks when unpredictable dictators surrounded her. With the benefit of hindsight, heroic courage would certainly have been appropriate, but it was the duty of those responsible at the time to weigh the risks carefully, which is precisely what they did.

The End of the War

Those pointing a finger at Switzerland have also criticized the people who were then in responsible positions for not having entered into the war by the winter of 1944/45, in other words, for not having formally declared war on Germany, as many other countries in the world had. If she had done this, Switzerland would have become automatically a member of the United Nations organization.

There was no question of this in 1945. Switzerland was continuing to abide by her neutrality, even though this presented more drawbacks than advantages. In addition, she was exhausted by the duration of the conflict and her sustained efforts, but there was also the worrying question as to whether she would escape the horrors of the war.

It was, therefore, a feeling of immense and common gratitude that the Swiss people shared on May 8, 1945, marking the end of the war in Europe. This feeling led to the "Swiss Gift" which collected some 200 million Swiss francs, belying the image of a self-centered Switzerland, although today some people are seeking to conceal this.[19]

The Washington Agreement

The feeling of gratitude that filled Switzerland in 1945 was quickly replaced by bitter findings. The victors had scarcely any consideration for the small neutral state that had contributed in no way to the downfall of Hitler. The Soviet Union turned down the proposition to reestablish diplomatic relations with such a typically bourgeois country. The Americans blocked Swiss assets in the United States as well as the National Bank's gold deposits there. They also maintained "blacklists" of Swiss companies that had traded for too long with Germany. In relative terms, Switzerland had become even smaller, as former major powers like France had been reduced to the status of medium sized states by comparison with the United States and the USSR. In other words, what had been grateful friendship towards the major powers turned into a feeling of fear.

In this context, the perspective of improving relations with the victorious countries through negotiations in Washington in 1946 brought hope. Minister Walter Stucki and his colleagues managed to find a bearable arrangement for Switzerland after relentless negotiations. Against payment of 250 million Swiss francs on May 25, 1946, Switzerland obtained formal assurance that any claims made against her would be dropped.

Conclusion

Switzerland's image during the Second World War was not one of a small heroic state sacrificing herself in the fight against tyranny, nor

---

[19] The figure of 200 million Swiss francs was considerable, considering the annual gross national product was about 10 billion Swiss francs at that time.

was it of a willing partner to Nazi Germany (as was Austria). Switzerland stood by her neutrality in a bid for survival.[20] Her sympathies were with the Western Allies, but she had to come to a compromise with Germany and Italy. This was the only way she could survive and – helped by business from Germany – stave off impending unemployment. Certainly, there were small minorities who did sympathize with Nazi Germany. However, the vast majority of the people felt a deep loathing for Germany as she was then. This feeling has persisted to the present day in the older generations.[21] From today's viewpoint, some of the measures taken at the time could be criticized, but this should not detract from the fact that a small democratic country encircled by dictators managed to survive. Any objective observer will admit that this itself was an impressive feat.

---

[20] Churchill was perhaps not mistaken when he commented to his Secretary of Foreign Affairs that of all the neutral countries, Switzerland deserved the most recognition.

[21] One may mention here the increased popularity of dialect in the German part of Switzerland, where it has become the language of oral communication in all daily events. Even if there are other reasons for this, this linguistic assertion is probably not without links to the allergy to Nazi Germany.

CONTRIBUTORS AND ACKNOWLEDGMENTS

Essays by the following contributors were originally published in German as part of an omnibus volume by the Verlag Neue Zürcher Zeitung (NZZ) in 1997 with the title *Der Zweite Weltkrieg und die Schweiz.* Permission to publish them in English was generously granted by the publisher NZZ and by the authors. Unless otherwise noted, these essays were translated by Lotti N. Eichhorn and adapted by John Gardner and Leo Schelbert.

Hugo Bütler – Chief Editor, NZZ

Prologue: Swiss History under Scrutiny was originally entitled Schweizer Vergangenheit auf dem Prüfstand. Mr. Bütler's second essay Neutral Switzerland – Humanitarian Switzerland: A Contradiction? was originally entitled Neutrale Schweiz – humanitäre Schweiz: Ein Widerspruch?

Walther Hofer – Historian, Professor Emeritus, University of Bern

Who Prolonged the Second World War? was originally entitled Wer hat wann den Zweiten Weltkrieg verlängert? The English translation, reproduced in this volume, was published in the *Swiss Review of World Affairs*, August 1997.

Hans Schaffner – Formerly Director of the Central Office for War Economy, Federal Councilor and President of Switzerland

Switzerland's Foreign Trade Policy during World War Two: Successful Perseverance of a Besieged Country was originally entitled Die Aussenhandelspolitik der Schweiz im Zweiten Weltkrieg: Erfolgreicher Durchhaltkampf eines verflochtenen Landes.

Dieter Schindler – Professor of International Law, University of Zürich

Contested Swiss Neutrality was originally entitled Umstrittene Neutralität: Anerkennung und Kritik in der Kriegs- und Nachkriegszeit. The author generously provided the English translation of his essay reproduced in this volume.

Hans Senn – Historian and former Chief of the General Staff of the Swiss Army

The Swiss Army was Ready: Reasons Germany Dropped "Operation Switzerland" was originally entitled Die Schweizer Armee stand bereit: Gründe für den Verzicht auf die vorbereitete "Operation Schweiz."

Klaus Urner – Professor and Director of Contemporary History Archives, Federal Institute of Technology, Zürich.

Neutrality and Economic Warfare was originally entitled Neutralität und Wirtschaftskrieg: Wie die Abschnürung durch Blockade und Gegenblockade verhindert wurde.

Essays by the following contributors are also included in this volume.

Detlef F. Vagts – Professor of International Law, Harvard Law School

Switzerland, International Law and World War Two was published as an Editorial Comment in *The American Journal of International Law* Vol. 91, No. 3, July 1997, 466-475. This article is reproduced with permission from *The American Journal of International Law*,© The American Society of International Law.

Sigmund Widmer – Formerly Mayor of the City of Zürich and National Councilor.

Epilogue: Summary View of Switzerland in World War Two was published in English with the title Switzerland and the Second World War in *Réflexions*, Number XVIII, 1999 by Darier Hentsch & Cie, Private Bankers. It was an abridged translation of Die Schweiz: Ein klärender und objektiver Blick auf ihre Vergangenheit, prepared by the author for the think tank Groupe de Réflexion Suisse-Europe. Permission to reproduce this translation was graciously granted by the Bank.

INDEX

prepared by Picton Press

ALPHAND
--, 39
ALTERMATT
Urs, 20
BADOGLIO
Marshal, 81
BERBER
Friedrich, 99
BERGIER
Jean-François, 37
BIERI
Josef, 42
BINDSCHEDLER
Rudolf, 101
BINSWANGER
H C, 36
Blockades, vi, ix, xii,
4, 6-8, 12-13, 16-17,
19, 24-27, 29-31,
41-48, 50-51, 56,
58-59, 71, 81, 88
BLUMENTRITT
--, 82
BOECKLE
Willi A, 77
BOLLIGER
Kurt, 101
BONJOUR
--, 51-53, 55, 57-58
Edgar, 38, 59, 101
BÖSCHENSTEIN
Hermann, 15, 45

BRANDELL
Ulf, 102
BRINER
Hans Rudolf, 27
BRUNS
--, 49
Victor, 48
Viktor, 48
BUCHER
Erwin, 108
BÜHRLE
Emil, 44
BÜTLER
Hugo, v-vii, ix, 87,
131
CARLGREN
Wilhelm, 21
CHAMBERLAIN
Neville, 78
CHURCHILL
--, vii, xv, 82, 90,
129
Winston, ix-x, xiii,
79, 114-115
Cold war, x, 96-97,
104
CORNAZ
Max, 35
Counterblockades, vi,
xii, 4, 9, 11-12, 16,
22-23, 26-28, 44, 49,
53-56, 71, 106

CUENDET
Georges-André, 117
CURRIE
Lauchlin, 58, 93
D'AMATO, xi, xiv,
89
DASHICHEV
Vyachislav I, 80
DUNANT
Henri, 87
DURRER
Marco, 27, 58-59
EDEN
Anthony, 114
EHRBAR
Hans Rudolf, 35
EICHHORN
Lotti N, 131
EISENHOWER
--, 81-83
EIZENSTAT
--, xiv, 92-93, 97
Stuart, xiii
Stuart E, vii, 91
Eizenstat Report, vi,
ix, xii, 81, 91, 93, 96
FAVEZ
Jean-Claude, 77, 108
FEISST
Ernst, 20
FIERZ
--, 40, 43

135

FODOR
Denis J, 103
FREI
Daniel, 58
FRÖHLICHER
--, 23, 43-44
FUHRER
--, 51
Hans Rudolf, 51
FÜHRER
--, 66-67
FULLER
--, 82
J F C, 81, 83
FUNK
Walter, 21, 105
GARAMVÖLGYI
J, 20
GARDNER
John, 131
GIBBELS
Ellen, 67
GORDON
David, 56
GÖRING
--, 42, 53
GRÜNINGER
Paul, 111
GUISAN
--, 64-65, 68, 70,
119, 122
Henri, 40, 119
GYSSLER
George, viii
HACKWORTH
--, 105
HAGGLÖF
Gunnar, 21
HAUG
H, 36

HEMMEN
--, 22, 41-44, 46, 54
Johannes Richard,
22
HILBERG
Raul, 110
HILLGRUBER
Andreas, 83
HILTY
Donald P, viii
HIMMLER
Heinrich, 7
HITLER
--, ix-x, xii-xv, 10,
66-70, 75, 77, 80-
81, 83, 87-90,
101-102, 106-107,
119, 121, 123,
125, 127-128
HOBI
Cassian, 28
HOFER
Walther, vi, 76, 79,
131
HOMBERGER
--, 18, 22, 51, 57,
114
Heinrich, 17, 49,
106
Heinrich III, 48, 56
HOTZ
Jean, 43, 49
HUBER
Max, 117
HURNI
Peter, 36
Information Void, v
JAEGGI
André, 37

JÄGER
Jörg-Johannes, 20
Jews/ Jewish, x, 87,
94, 108-111, 124-
126
KARBOM
Rolf, 20
KELLER
Paul, 57
KELLY
David, 40
KÖCHER
--, 54, 70
KOECHLIN
C E, 49
KOHLI
R, 49
Robert, 48-49, 57
KUNZ
Josef L, 99
KURZ
Hans Rudolf, 31
LAHOUSEN
--, 51
LAMB
Richard, 107
LENIN
--, 123
LIPPMANN
Walter, 79
LOMAX
--, 57
LUCIRI
Pierre, 30
LÜTHY
Herbert, xiv
MARGUERAT
--, 73(2)
P, 67

MEDLICOTT
W N, 47
MEIER
Heinz K, 19
MILWARD
Alan S, 20
MINGER
Rudolf, 78
MITCHELL
--, 25, 29
B R, 24
MOLOTOV
Vyacheslav M, 80
MONTGOMERY
--, 82-83
MOTTA
Giuseppe, 117
MUSSOLINI
--, xii-xiii, 81
NAPOLEON
--, 77
OBRECHT
--, 45-48
Hermann, 39
OCHSENBEIN
Heinz, 30
OCHSNER
--, 104
Richard, 103
PACKARD
Jerrold M, 105
PAUL
Randolph, 113
PERRET
Geoffrey, 103
PICARD
--, 111
Jacques, 109
PILET-GOLAZ
--, 38, 70
Marcel, 122

RAPPARD
William E, 96
RIKLIN
A, 36
RINGS
--, 105, 112
Werner, 58, 102
ROESCH
Werner, 102
ROESLE
Eugen, 18
ROOSEVELT
--, 93
Franklin D, 79
Theodore, 107
SANDLER
Richard, 36
SAUSER-HALL
Georges, 112
SCHAFFNER
Hans, vi, 3, 15, 131
SCHELBERT
Leo, viii, 131
SCHELLENBERG
--, 70
SCHINDLER
D, 49
Dieter, vii, 132
Dietrich, 49, 91,
100, 112
SCHWARZ
Urs, 36
SENN
Hans, vi, 63, 75,
102, 132
SEYBOTH
--, 22, 49
SIMÉON
--, 40
SPEER
--, 78

Albert, 77
SPEIDEL
--, 82
SPEISER
Ernst, 17-18
STALIN
--, 80-81, 107, 123
STAMM
--, 108
Konrad, 107
STAMPFLI
--, 58
STREIT
Christian, 108
STUCKI
Walter, 128
SULZER
Hans, 57
Switzerland
accidental bombing
by United States,
103
Allied assistance,
xiii-xv, 11-12, 40,
42, 73, 104
Army, vi, xii, xiv-
xv, 4, 39-41, 53,
63-70, 72, 74-75,
103, 119, 132
Congress of Vienna,
xi, 101
democracy, xi, xiv,
89, 93
Federal Council, vi,
xi, 10, 13, 24, 30,
32-41, 43, 45-47,
50-51, 56-58, 64,
66-70, 87, 117,
120, 122-124, 131

Switzerland *cont'd*
Gold transactions,
vii, xii, 20, 22, 57-
58, 73-74, 77, 87-
88, 95-96, 106,
111-113, 115,
127-128
Government, vii,
xiv, 11, 16-17, 29-
30, 32-35, 37, 40-
41, 45, 55, 57, 59,
68, 70, 76, 79, 88-
89, 94-95, 99, 104,
106, 109, 111-114,
120
languages, 90, 129
Mobilization in, 40,
64, 118-120
Neutrality and
humanity, 99
Neutrality and
International Law,
vii, xiii, 31-32, 48,
99-100, 110-115
Neutrality contested
91, 132
Payments to Allies,
ix, xi, 17, 39, 53

Public Opinion, xi,
122
Redoubt, vi, x, xii, 4,
64-67, 69, 74,
122-123
Refugees, haven for,
xv, 87, 89-90, 94-
95, 108, 110-111,
124-126
Trade policy, vi, 3,
5, 7-8, 10, 13-14,
16-19, 21-22, 24,
30-31, 44, 50, 55,
59, 131
Transit routes, vi,
67, 69, 73-75
TANNER
Jacob, 76, 78
TANSILL
Charles C, 99
TOBLER
R, 123
TREFOUSSE
Hans L, 99
UKENA
Wolf, 36
URNER
--, 107

K, 19
Klaus, vi, 15, 44, 58,
105, 132
VAGTS
Detlef F, 132
Detlev F, xiii, 99
Prof, vii
VOGLER
Robert, 58
Robert U, 42
VON RUNDSTEDT
--, 82
WAHLEN
Friedrich T, 20
WALLENBERG
Raoul, 109
WHITTLESEY
Faith, viii, 78
WIDMER
Sigmund, vii, 117,
133
WILMOT
Chester, 82
WITTMANN
--, 21, 25
Klaus, 20
ZIEGLER
--, 77
Jean, 76